The
Political
South

in the Twentieth Century

MONROE LEE BILLINGTON

The
Political
South
in the Twentieth Century

CHARLES SCRIBNER'S SONS   NEW YORK

Copyright © 1975 Monroe Lee Billington

Library of Congress Cataloging in Publication Data

Billington, Monroe Lee.
　　The political South in the twentieth century.

　　Bibliography: p.
　　1. Southern States—Politics and government—1865–
1950. 2. Southern States—Politics and government—
1951–　　3. Negroes—Southern States. I. Title.
F215.B56　　　320.9′75′04　　　73-1312
ISBN 0-684-13983-9
ISBN 0-684-13986-3 (pbk.)

1 3 5 7 9 11 13 15 17 19 c/c 20 18 16 14 12 10 8 6 4 2
1 3 5 7 9 11 13 15 17 19 c/p 20 18 16 14 12 10 8 6 4 2

Printed in the United States of America

To Mary Elizabeth
and the 19,632 members of the League of
Women Voters in the eleven southern states who
love the South and want to improve it

Contents

Preface

Monographs and scholarly and popular articles on twentieth-century southern politics and politicians abound. Political scientists, sociologists, historians, journalists, and others have delved into the fascinating complexities of this subject. The finished products of their work have usually dealt with a particular state, or a specific politician, or a sharply limited time span. V. O. Key (*Southern Politics in State and Nation*) approached the subject from a broader perspective, but the work of this political scientist is now over twenty years old. More recently, William C. Havard has edited a large volume (*The Changing Politics of the South*), but it emphasizes the very recent South, and its organization of one chapter per state, each written by a different author, has its limitations. Clearly there is a place for a brief, general, up-to-date, interpretive account of southern politics in the twentieth century. This volume is intended to fill that need.

For the purposes of this volume, the South is defined as the eleven former Confederate states. I make occasional references to border states such as Maryland, Kentucky, and Oklahoma, but only when the reference is both necessary and relevant. I have avoided using the negative term non-South when I refer to the United States exclusive of the South. Rather I have used the traditional term North when I speak of the remainder of the nation, even though that term is not precisely accurate in every instance.

The bibliographical essay at the end of the volume constitutes my thanks to the writers whose works I have read and used. Thomas D. Clark led me into southern history years ago, and I much appreciate his interest in my writings generally and in this volume specifically. I want to thank my colleagues Simon Kropp and Gene Brack for reading the entire manuscript and for giving me their valuable critical judgments. For forcing me to rethink, rewrite, and reorganize large passages of early drafts, I am obligated to Elsie Kearns, Barbara Wood, and an unknown colleague, all employed by Charles Scribner's Sons. Margarete Vargo and Kay Davis patiently and accurately typed the manuscript. These words of thanks do not absolve me from full responsibility for errors in fact and interpretation.

Introduction

After the Civil War, southern blacks and northern Republicans controlled the politics of the South; but throughout Reconstruction when these newly enfranchised blacks and carpetbaggers (and some southern whites called scalawags) were in power, once-powerful southern Democrats were working to regain their prewar status. Between 1869 and 1877 these Democrats "redeemed" the eleven former Confederate states as they overthrew the Reconstruction governments and established themselves in preeminent political positions. The Redeemers (also called Restorationists, Brigadiers, and Bourbons) dominated southern politics until the end of the nineteenth century.

Although the Redeemers were mainly conservative Democrats, prewar Whigs comprised a significant minority of the group. When the Whig party died out in the 1850s and was replaced with the Republican party, southern Whigs faced a dilemma. Before the Civil War they could not join the Republicans, who were committed to oppose the extension of slavery into American territories; but they were too proud to be affiliated with southern Democrats, their longtime political enemies. The Republican party could have appealed to these southern Whigs during the Reconstruction era—after the slavery question had been settled—but it preferred instead to build its strength in the South on black voters. This policy, coupled with their common economic conservatism, led southern Whigs to swallow their pride and join the Democrats to "redeem" the South, dominating its politics thereafter and preventing or restricting black political involvement. For a number of years one-party politics prevailed, and during the ascendancy of the Redeemers, frugality, reduced public services, economic retrenchment, and efforts to control black voter participation characterized state governments.

The solidarity of the South was disturbed at the end of the nineteenth century when agrarian discontent prompted middle- and lower-class southerners to resist the political and economic supremacy of the Redeemers. These Agrarians needed whatever political support they could find, and they made overt appeals to the scattered Republicans throughout the South as well as to blacks. The combination gave the southern wing of the Populist party enough strength to challenge the Democrats during the first half of the 1890s. Because it crossed class and racial lines, this type of "fusion" politics was fraught with dangers; but conditions were such that the Agrarians were willing to go to extremes to oust the Redeemers. The possibility of black men holding power in the southern states still frightened whites, however; so when their Populist zeal was quenched in 1896 and the shaky coalition fell apart, white southerners set out with even greater determination to keep blacks out of the voting booths and to prevent them from holding public office.

The characteristics of the so-called Solid South—the dominance of conservative Democrats and former Whigs, the weakness of the Republican organization, and white southerners' fear of the potential political power of blacks—remained in the years after 1900; but significant differences appeared early in the new century, and others developed as time passed. Progressive Democrats were able to compete successfully with the conservatives in the early twentieth century, giving the solidly Democratic South a political factionalism that resembled two-party conditions. Both Progressives and conservatives agreed that blacks should not be involved in the political process, and they continued the Redeemer tradition of repression. The national movement for black civil and political rights after the Second World War affected even the South, however, and by the 1970s blacks were much involved in regional politics. At the same time, economic and social changes were altering the South, creating fertile conditions for the growth of the Republican party. By the 1970s the region had changed so much politically that it could no longer accurately be referred to as "solid." Blacks still do not have full political power and a two-party system does not yet exist in every state, but progress along those lines has been made. One hundred years after Reconstruction the South is far along the road back to the mainstream of biracial, two-party American national politics.

The
Political
South
in the Twentieth Century

ONE

Progressive
Politics

The hopes of the Progressive movement in the United States were perhaps too extensive to be realized in their entirety. Yet that movement was an extraordinarily attractive development in American life, and in no part of the country did it find more enthusiasm than in the South. The South's conservative political and social course in the post–Civil War era had caused leading Progressives such as Wisconsin's Senator Robert M. La Follette and the Kansas newspaperman William Allen White to assume that the Progressive movement had bypassed the region. For many years this assumption has been accepted without question by political leaders, commentators, even historians. Recent study, however, has revealed that the South was very much a part of that important movement, that the spirit of reform quickened many southerners and their leaders. The South had a Progressive side to its ways of behavior that reflected southern attitudes, and it was clearly evident during the years after the turn of this century.

1

PROGRESSIVE
SOUTHERNERS

Historians traditionally have dated the Progressive era in the United States from September 1901, when Theodore Roosevelt took the oath of office as president, to April 1917, when the nation's entry into the First World War submerged the reform impulse. The Progressive movement was a notable response to the country's industrialization in the last years of the nineteenth century; its disciples believed that government had the responsibility to control or direct this economic expansion. They rejected nineteenth-century laissez-faire determinism, and they believed that the government should act as an agency of human welfare. Between the turn of the century and the nation's entry into the war, Progressives were successful in securing a few of their specific objectives, such as legislation that established a modern national banking system, commissions to regulate transportation and manufacturing, and an income tax to help finance larger government. Progressives also hoped to root out graft and corruption in high places by infusing government with more democracy; thus, they instituted direct election of United States senators, female suffrage, the direct primary, initiative, and referendum. In view of the growth of industry with its attendant evils for many Americans, the Progressives desired not only to control business expansion but to ensure a more healthy personal development; in some areas of the country, militant Progressives managed to outlaw the sale of alcoholic beverages.

Like the rest of the country, the South had been touched by industrialization and visited by the increasing financial difficulties —banking, lending, currency—of the years after the Civil War, and the ideas of the Progressives were therefore highly attractive. A spirit of reform was clearly in evidence by the turn of the century. The South admittedly was far from a perfect democratic society; with great sincerity southern political leaders undertook to improve conditions in their section. The active reformers in the South generally came from urban and middle-class backgrounds and were usually city or small-town professionals and businessmen. They held views similar to those of their northern counterparts, favoring governmental centralization, more federal power, better public services, and regulation of corporations for fairer and more effective competition. But southern progressivism also embraced an element of agrarianism not present in the northern Progressive doctrine. During the Populist era of the 1880s and 1890s, southern farmers had begun to demand more democratic political practices, the dismantling of monopolistic trusts, protection of local agrarian interests, and governmental decentralization. Although their interests overlapped rather than coincided, these rural southerners joined with urban Progressives to oppose a common enemy in the early 1900s, bringing a unique and distinct flavor to the Progressive movement in the South.

The enemy was economic dependency. The Bourbons of the late nineteenth century had allied themselves with the wealthy interests of the North and East, placing the South in the position of an economic colony. Banks, insurance companies, public utilities, oil companies, pipelines, textile mills, tobacco manufacturers, and jute-bagging companies exploited the southerner and his area's resources. Railroads were particularly blatant in their abuses, and Progressives singled them out for attacks. Small businessmen and farmers who were struggling to make a living depended on the railroad. They were painfully conscious of the cuts in their incomes caused by transportation bills when they shipped products to market or when they purchased supplies.

Southern politicians were receptive to criticism of trusts and corporations that were not acting "in the public interest," and many were elected to office in the early 1900s, having pledged to control the giant industries. Braxton Bragg Comer, as a merchant, manufacturer, and shipper, was aware of the high rates charged by railroads; in his successful campaign for the governorship of Alabama he opposed rate discrimination. In response to Governor Comer's pressure, the Alabama legislature passed a comprehensive railway code that greatly expanded the authority of the state railroad commission, increased tax rates on railroad-owned property, reduced shipping and passenger rates, prohibited lobbying, and banned passes for public officials. As a "friend of the people," Governor James K. Vardaman of Mississippi championed the farmer's case against "predatory" corporations. Believing that "money interests" ruled the world, he viewed banks and railroads as insects that devoured the farmer by usurious rates and exorbitant tariffs; he favored reduction of interest rates and establishment of state and federal railroad commissions. At his urging the state legislature passed laws to supervise railroads, public utilities, banks, manufacturers, trusts, and insurance companies. Vardaman's protégé and successor, Theodore ("The

Man") Bilbo, extended the tradition by setting up a state highway commission. With Governor Hoke Smith's encouragement, the Georgia legislature passed a corrupt practices act, a measure reducing train passenger rates, and a law abolishing passes on railroads and adjusting freight schedules downward. It had already established a state railroad commission in 1879, one of the earliest state regulatory bodies in the nation; in 1907, largely because of Smith's persistence, the legislature reorganized the commission and greatly expanded its jurisdiction. A veritable pattern of state regulation developed throughout the South during the Progressive era.

Perhaps no southern governor fought harder against corporate abuse than did Jeff Davis of Arkansas. As the state's attorney general, he had instituted some 225 suits against fire insurance companies operating in the state, and as governor he continued his efforts to place restrictions on the insurance companies, life as well as fire, which he believed would protect the policyholders and the public. From 1901 to 1905 the Arkansas legislature passed nine laws that literally drove insurance companies out of the state. As attorney general, Davis had also sued the Standard Oil Company, the American Tobacco Company, the "Cotton Seed Oil Trust," and the express companies. As governor he sponsored a series of acts designed to break the power of the trusts and other corporations, or at least to protect the public.

Of all areas of southern life needing reform, education was one of the most desperate. By any standards the quality of public schools in the South was poor. They were miserably supported, incompetently staffed, and totally inadequate for the region's needs. The national average for expenditure per pupil in the 1900–1901 school year was $21.14, but not a single southern state spent as much as half that amount. Instruction was deplorable; fewer than a fifth of all elementary school teachers had a high school education and fewer than half had even a modicum of professional training. Teachers earned an average of $159 per school year in the South, half the national average. While the average length of school terms in the whole country was 145 days in 1900–1901, the southern states averaged only 96 days, and rural districts considerably less than that. Fewer than half of all southern children attended school regularly. The dropout rate was appalling: for every seventy pupils who enrolled in the first grade, only seven reached the fifth grade and only one got to the eighth.

Such conditions prompted some northern philanthropists to

Two views of child labor, which the Progressives sought to regulate through legislation. *Right:* "Business Opportunity in the Cotton Mills. See 'Help Wanted' in the Next Morning's Papers." (*Life*, 12 February 1914). *Below:* Lewis W. Hine photograph, 1909. "Some of the so-called 'helpers' in a Georgia cotton mill who were so small they had to climb onto the frames of the machine to reach." (International Museum of Photography at George Eastman House)

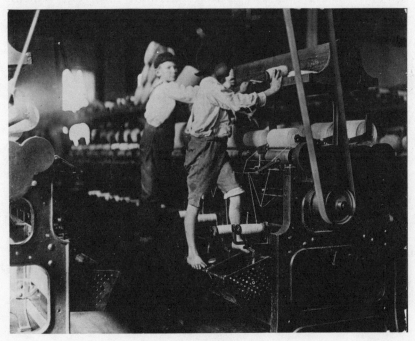

establish a southern education fund in 1902, and during the next seven years millions of dollars (mainly from Rockefeller money) were poured into the South's schools. To supplement this private support, Progressive southern governors and their legislatures founded educational institutions, erected new school buildings to replace inadequate ones, and provided free textbooks for children attending public schools. At Governor Napoleon B. Broward's recommendation, the Florida legislature created a board of control for its state's institutions of higher learning; Governor Vardaman persuaded the Mississippi legislature to increase funds for schools; Governor Davis established public libraries and set up graded courses in Arkansas's school system. Governor Comer induced the Alabama legislature to establish county high schools that became the foundation of the state's secondary school system. Governor Charles B. Aycock's consuming passion was education for all North Carolinians. He encouraged his legislature to pass a new school code, reorganize the state's educational system, hire more qualified teachers and administrators, and appropriate more money for public education. In Alabama and North Carolina, Progressive educational reforms were the most successful among all the states of the South.

The governors and legislatures did not favor every major Progressive reform, but these measures frequently passed: unfair practices laws, child labor legislation, safety and inspection procedures for mills and mines, pure food and drug laws, penal reform measures (including abolition of the convict-lease system), and appropriations for charitable institutions. Several Progressive administrations built bridges and public highway systems, and more than one governor rooted out graft and corruption in the bureaucracy of his state. Because the South was the most formally religious section of the nation, southerners generally favored Prohibition, a nineteenth-century crusade that successfully tied itself to progressivism after the turn of the century. Hoke Smith guided a Prohibition bill through his legislature in 1907, making Georgia the first southern state to adopt statewide Prohibition.

The failures of the South during the Progressive era should not, of course, be overlooked, for the full Progressive program was not often realized. Andrew Jackson Montague of Virginia worked for Progressive reforms, but he was notably unsuccessful. A legislature dominated by an anti-Montague faction and Montague's own political ineptness prevented the governor from carrying out most of his proposals. Other reform governors, such

as Florida's Park Trammel, were stymied by recalcitrant legislators. The Progressive movement in the South was slowed when
some governors, such as South Carolina's Coleman L. Blease,
after endorsing Progressive measures during their campaigns,
failed to press for reform legislation while in office.

After some southern Progressives were established in office,
they often failed to represent the poorer classes who had elected
them. It was not unusual for them to make peace with the
conservative planters and business interests they had so violently
attacked in their campaign tirades; rebellious attitudes softened
after elections. Part of the reason for double-talk related to the
great game of politics as played in the South. Politicians there had
long been adept at using current crises to win elections, after
which they gave little or no attention to those problems. Some of
the so-called reformers were no exception. But to criticize
unsuccessful reformers as being politically inspired is to do the
group as a whole a disservice. An urban-based liberalism that
might have strengthened their position did not exist, and the
South's paucity of urban centers was undoubtedly partly responsible for the limited success of the southern Progressives.

Another reason lay in the fact that they shared political power
with conservative opponents. The Progressives did not always win
political campaigns, and their lesser-known, more conservative
opponents often alternated in office. As heirs of the late nineteenth-century Bourbons, these old-line conservative politicians
reflected the attitudes of many of their constituents more accurately than did the Progressives.

Georgia politics revealed a classic Progressive-conservative
political confrontation. Joseph M. Brown was a prototype of all
the South's conservative Democrats who vied with reformers
during the Progressive era. Brown was the son of a member of the
Bourbon triumvirate that had included Alfred H. Colquitt and
John B. Gordon and had dominated Georgia politics after
Reconstruction. In the tradition of his father, the younger Brown
was sympathetic to the railroad interests, to industry, and to the
large insurance companies whose headquarters were in Atlanta.
After being employed by the Western and Atlantic Railroad for
over twenty years, he was appointed to the Georgia railroad
commission in 1904. He got his first political notice in 1907, when
Governor Smith accused him of not carrying out his commission
duties and criticized him for opposing the reduction of passenger
rates. When Brown prepared an eighty-page pamphlet, which the

railroads subsequently circulated, arguing against the reductions, Smith removed him from the commission, whereupon Brown wrote an elaborate critique of "reformers." A few months later, with the support of important leaders of Georgia's conservative Democrats, he announced his candidacy for the governorship. He won in 1908 on a conservative platform, having advocated reduced taxes, restriction of the railroad commission's powers, and encouragement of out-of-state investments.

One-party politics has never meant that battles do not occur. Elections in the South were often quiet formalities because of the weakness of the state Republican parties, but such could not be said of southern Democratic primaries. Occasionally several candidates entered the Democratic primaries, but there were often only two serious contenders—usually designated by the conservative and Progressive wings of the party. The Smith-Brown feud in Georgia was an example of this bifactionalism. Smith pulled together the reform elements of the Democratic party in Georgia and made them into a powerful group; Brown was the candidate of such conservatives as Clark Howell, the longtime editor of the *Atlanta Constitution.* At a time when reform was in the air in a state pledged to tradition, political battles occurred with regularity.

Politics in Georgia during the Progressive era took on an interesting dimension because of the local presence of Thomas E. Watson, an agrarian rebel during the Populist period. Watson had risen high enough in Populist ranks to be nominated for the vice-presidency in 1896. Despite populism's rapid decline he was able to retain his small-farmer power base and continued to dominate Georgia politics. His support for Smith's 1906 bid for the governorship was crucial. Watson was undoubtedly influential in pushing Smith to the political left, perhaps further toward progressivism than Smith had intended to go. When the governor seemed less reform-minded than Watson desired, this fascinating political maverick threw his support to the conservative Brown. Many of Watson's followers could not bring themselves to vote for Brown, but Watson's opposition to Smith defeated the governor. The fact that both the Smith and Brown factions worked to win or retain Watson's support during the campaign is indicative of his political clout. Watson returned to the Democratic party in 1910 after a twenty-year absence, although during that period he had had more influence upon state politics than any other person. The inveterate independent then dominated the party at the state level for another decade, but he acknowledged no allegiance to the national organization. In 1912 he impishly voted for Theodore Roosevelt and the Bull Moose ticket, although he was still boss of the Democratic party in Georgia.

Southern politics during the Progressive era embodied all sorts of contradictions and even apparent absurdities; no single generalization can explain them. Differences between the Progressives and conservatives were not as pronounced as those customary terms may indicate. Members of both groups often favored antilobbying laws as well as regulation of railroads and public utilities, and their support for improved education tended further to blur any distinct categorizations. Although Prohibition was eventually associated with progressivism, conservative leaders also favored it for religious reasons, because of the antialcoholism in the Protestant South. Yet the Progressives and conservatives appealed to distinctly different groups. By soliciting the support of the common southerner, the resident of the small town, the hill farmer, the poor white in Atlanta or in Mobile, the Progressives proclaimed a new era in southern politics. After the long years of the post–Civil War supremacy of the Bourbons, the Progressive coalition of small planters, merchants, and lawyers undertook to revolutionize southern state politics. It is understandable why the underprivileged whites in the hills and the piney woods sections of the South responded favorably. "You can look at the back of my neck and see that I am a Vardaman man," a Mississippian said in 1910. Progressives with their redneck followers seized control of their state governments from the delta and black-belt planters and their business allies. Even when the Progressives did not keep promises to the poor farmers, they generally retained the support of these southerners who had formerly been little involved in politics. One farmer's statement, "I know Blease don't do no more for us than them other fellers but at least it's one of us that ain't doing nothing," indicates the spirit, at least, of reform. The Progressive leaders, even the less effective ones, served as a safety valve for the discontented. Even if they did not win every election, they became powerful enough to contend with the old guard southern leaders, and southern politics would never again be the same. Indeed, the Progressives laid the foundation of democracy in later southern politics.

SOUTHERN RACISTS

Racism simmered just under the surface of the American scene in the last quarter of the nineteenth century, and it boiled over in the South as the century came to a close. By the 1890s the United States had acquired what was nearly an empire; the Americans' obligation to care for a share of the world's brown people was the justification for acquisition. The nation masked its economic interest in the Philippine Islands and elsewhere with the "doctrine" of the White Man's Burden. Writers such as Josiah Strong popularized belief in Anglo-Saxon superiority, and white Americans rationalized their nation's actions in the name of Christianity. During the same period white polemicists published a rash of ultraracist books, such as *The Negro a Beast* (1900) and *The Negro: A Menace to Civilization* (1907). *Birth of a Nation*, a melodramatic movie glorifying white superiority and emphasizing black racial degradation, appealed to the same racist instincts.

In the late nineteenth century, the federal courts, the government in Washington, northern liberal opinion, and moderate southerners had forced extreme southerners to suppress their fears, jealousies, hatreds, and fanaticism toward blacks, but these restraining forces were dissipated after the turn of the century. As the nation acquired and ruled its empire, the courts and the federal government sympathized with the theory of white superiority. Northern liberals were disposed to be less critical of southern racial attitudes in an era when the doctrine of Anglo-Saxon superiority was in vogue and when the nation was assuming the White Man's Burden around the world.

In view of the national intellectual milieu and the lessening of restraints, white southerners no longer felt the necessity of controlling their fear and hatred of blacks. Reflecting the spirit of the times, southern state legislatures and municipalities adopted laws and ordinances proscribing black activity. Unwritten laws, regulations, customs, and traditions were formalized before the First World War. This drive for white control of black activity was nowhere more apparent than in the political arena. In view of the legacy of carpetbag Reconstruction, Bourbon rule, racial tension during the Populist era, and the nationwide increase of a feeling of white superiority, the prospect of black participation in the democratic political process distressed southerners, who worked diligently to prevent it.

Southern politicians were almost unanimous in their desire for black disfranchisement. Political campaigns in the early 1900s often became contests of who could make the strongest antiblack statements on the hustings. In order to compete successfully with the dominant conservative Democratic factions of machines, southern Progressive Democrats did not hesitate to appeal to racial prejudice. The vehemence of their campaigns acquired for them the label of "demagogues." Because they were often the "outs" wanting to replace the "ins," however, Progressives had to resort to violent oratory that would outdo their opponents; they were not alone in their exploitation of racial fears.

Mississippi adopted the direct primary in 1902, and Vardaman secured the Democratic nomination for governor the next year. The fact that he had been denied the nomination twice until the direct primary went into effect is significant: to win the nomination in 1902 he had to appeal to the white masses rather than to the party's leaders, and the factor that would earn for him a majority of the votes was white concern for a resurgent black minority. Vardaman acknowledged approvingly that the question of blacks voting was not only a matter of fitness, "but rather a matter of race prejudice—as deep-seated and ineradicable as the Anglo-Saxon genius for self-government." He described the black man as an industrial stumbling block, a political ulcer, a social scab, "a lazy, lying, lustful animal which no conceivable amount of training can transform into a tolerable citizen." To Vardaman the black man's nature "resembles the hog's" rather than the white man's. He spoke of the black male's desires for white women and suggested that this passion be curbed by counter-violence. He even admitted that lynch law should prevail occasionally if a black needed to be punished. "We would be justified in slaughtering every Ethiop on the earth to preserve unsullied the honor of one Caucasian home." The only way the black could prosper was by avoiding politics and by maintaining "the relation which he now occupies to the white folks." Throughout his political career Vardaman did not move from the stated views in his early campaigns. To accentuate his support of white supremacy, Vardaman donned a white linen suit and campaigned in the Mississippi farmlands from the bed of a whitewashed lumber wagon drawn by white oxen—a symbolic gesture that Mississippi's illiterate farmers recognized and to which they responded favorably. In his successful bid for a U.S. Senate seat in 1907 in which the race question was the crucial issue, Vardaman advo-

cated repeal of Reconstruction amendments and argued that if
blacks were permitted to vote, fraud and violence would be
necessary to retain white supremacy.

Bilbo had widespread appeal based upon antiblack tirades,
the rising self-consciousness of the small farmers, and his own
eccentric personality. His tirades against his political opponents
and his knack for being in the middle of highly publicized verbal
feuds worked to his advantage as he appealed to the baser
sentiments of the rednecks and as his opponents accorded him
free publicity by their constant attacks. One newspaper editor
wrote that Bilbo "is attractive in the same way that freaks of
nature are regarded." He was said to use "language that would
shock a fishwoman," and he was variously described as "a
thorough rascal," "the whelp Bilbo," "a self-confessed bribe-
taker," "a frequenter of lewd houses," "a pimp," "a moral leper,"
"a vile degenerate," and "a low-flung scullion." But Bilbo himself
was without a peer in the use of invective; of an enemy he said,
"He was begotten iń a nigger graveyard at midnight, suckled by a
sow and educated by a fool." Bilbo came into physical combat
with his enemies on more than one occasion during his colorful
but undignified campaigns.

Hoke Smith's gubernatorial campaign of 1905–6 revealed the
rising racism in Georgia. He was the former publisher of the
Atlanta Journal and a member of President Grover Cleveland's
cabinet in the 1890s and had been a moderate on the race issue
before 1905. He had subscribed to white paternalism as the best
policy for blacks, advocating black education and opposing
disfranchisement. His widely circulated newspaper had condemned lynching as "inconsistent with proper reverence for the
law," and he had often praised Booker T. Washington and his
moderate racial stance. For whatever reasons, however—perhaps
political expediency—Smith added a disfranchisement plank to
his gubernatorial platform in 1905. In his attempts to appeal to
white voters, Smith in one of his campaign speeches said: "No
more important question can be presented to the people of
Georgia than the disfranchisement of the ignorant, purchasable
negro vote. . . . This is a white man's country, and we are all
agreed that not only in the state at large, BUT IN EVERY
COUNTY AND IN EVERY COMMUNITY the white man must
control by some means, or life could not be worth living. . . ." He
expressed "humiliation" over the fact that McIntosh County had

Movie still from *Birth of a Nation*: a Klan lynching. (Museum of Modern Art Film Stills Archives)

sent a black man to the state legislature, and he approved various southern states' constitutional provisions for white supremacy.

Race baiting in the political campaigns in the South was the obvious manifestation of the movement to disfranchise blacks by whatever legal and extralegal means were available. Southern political leaders of the early twentieth century were determined not only to exploit white prejudice to win elections, but also, once they attained office, to keep the black man completely out of politics. The success of the Progressives in attaining greater black disfranchisement was undoubtedly their most important long-range influence. Their firm opposition to black involvement in the democratic process was the result of many historical factors, the most immediate being the political events of the 1890s. In order to compete successfully with the dominant Democratic party, the newly formed Populist party had attempted to appeal to as many potential voting allies as possible. While the Populists "fused" their organization with the small Republican party in the South, they made covert appeals to the black voter. Seriously challenged for political supremacy for the first time since Reconstruction, southern conservative Democrats responded to Populist insurgency by making *sub rosa* appeals to black voters, too. Neither the established Democrats nor the middle- and lower-class Populists were eager to have more blacks involved in the political process, but each group recognized the high stakes in the political game of the nineties and for a few years they suppressed their misgivings. Blacks did not play a large role in the South's two-party years from 1890 to 1896, but that they were involved at all, and more importantly that they might in the future have a degree of political leverage, deeply troubled southern white men. Thus, when Populist candidates were defeated in the elections of 1896, white southern politicians almost to a man resolved to prevent blacks from ever becoming the political balance of power in the region. Without question one of the chief results of populism in the South was the stimulus it gave to black disfranchisement.

Southerners in the early twentieth century who were determined to disfranchise blacks had a solid base upon which to build. As southern whites had regained control of the various state governments at the end of the Reconstruction period, they had set about through various means to reduce the weight of the black vote. Included among the Bourbons' bag of tricks in one state or another were gerrymandering, poll taxes, changing elective offices to appointive ones, and careful control of the Democratic party machinery by whites. State legislatures passed laws that prohibited voting by persons convicted of certain crimes—clearly those most often committed by blacks—and they passed complex election laws to confuse the politically naïve black voters. The most famous of these was South Carolina's Eight Box Law, which required a separate ballot box for each office; when illiterate black voters placed their ballots in the wrong receptacle their votes were voided. In the 1890s several states amended their constitutions to require that each qualified voter be able to read a passage of the United States Constitution or to give a reasonable interpretation of a portion of it after it was read to him. Election officials were empowered to administer these literacy tests, and the result of their "discretionary" application was, of course, a decline in the black vote. After 1895 some states set up minimum property qualifications for voters as an alternative to the literacy requirement, but this benefited propertyless blacks little. In 1898 Louisiana added a "grandfather clause" to the state constitution to protect whites who might lose the vote because of literacy tests or property requirements. This amendment provided that anyone whose ancestor had voted before 1867 was not required to take the literacy test or meet property ownership stipulations. Suffrage was therefore available to poor white illiterates but closed to blacks, whose ancestors could not vote in Louisiana before the beginning of Radical Reconstruction in 1867.

Mississippi, South Carolina, and Louisiana led in inventing techniques for voiding the U.S. Constitution by state laws and state constitutional amendments. During the early years of the twentieth century, as racism and progressivism simultaneously swept across the section, other southern states adopted many of the same ways to disfranchise blacks, added refinements, and dreamed up additional devices to protect the white man's voting booth. Georgia, Florida, Mississippi, Tennessee, Arkansas, South Carolina, and Louisiana had adopted poll tax requirements before the turn of the century, and by 1908 laws in North Carolina, Alabama, Texas, and Virginia established the poll tax in every southern state. Each law had its own peculiarities. Some made the tax cumulative if a voter did not pay it in previous elections; others required payment months in advance of an election; all but Tennessee made payment a prerequisite for voting in Democratic primaries. Even though the tax was nominal, it was intended to discourage currency-impoverished and debt-ridden blacks from exercising their political rights. Also during the first decade of the new century, both Alabama and Virginia framed and effected new constitutions primarily designed to disfranchise blacks. North Carolina adopted an educational standard for all voters except those who qualified to register under its "grandfather clause," and Georgia ratified a constitutional amendment prescribing a literacy test. Later Georgia authorized the registration of illiterates "of good character" who could prove that they understood "the duties and obligations of citizenship under a republican form of government." The vague wording of this statute gave white election officials wide discretionary powers, the result being that many illiterate whites were added to the registration rolls while illiterate blacks were not. Georgia also adopted property ownership as another alternative to literacy; poor whites were of course more likely than poor blacks to have small amounts of property. Throughout the South white political leaders levied poll taxes, enforced literacy tests, and judged the property qualifications of those who wished to register; the result was that unqualified blacks were not permitted to register or vote, but equally unqualified whites were. Most blacks did not challenge this obvious discrimination; those who did were powerless to effect change.

Following Louisiana's lead, several states instituted "grandfather clauses," either as constitutional amendments or as statutes. Three years after the border state of Oklahoma joined the Union its legislature enacted a "grandfather law," but in *Guinn* v. *United States* (1915) the Supreme Court voided the statute, proclaiming that a state could not reestablish conditions existing before the ratification of the Fifteenth Amendment, which guaranteed the vote for the black man. By 1915, however, the time period had already expired in all the states in which qualified persons could register permanently under the "grandfather clauses"; the principal effect of the Court decision was merely to prevent states from establishing new time periods in which certain persons could be exempted from the effects of the clauses by permanently registering to vote.

None of the South's efforts to disfranchise blacks from the end of Reconstruction through the Progressive era were overtly racial. Careful not to violate the letter of the Fifteenth Amendment, southern laws and constitutional amendments made no specific reference to race, even though the intent was obvious. In 1902 a Mississippian explained in all seriousness how his state's constitutional convention of 1890 was careful not to discriminate: "Every provision in the Mississippi Constitution applies equally, and without any discrimination whatever, to both the white and negro races. Any assumption, therefore, that the purpose of the framers of the Constitution was ulterior, and dishonest, is gratuitous and cannot be sustained."

The southern states' disfranchisement movement from 1890 to 1910 resulted in the most impressive series of obstacles to voting in the history of democratic nations. But statutory and constitutional disfranchisement of blacks did not satisfy the white supremacists, for these were not as effective in controlling black voting behavior as they desired. Furthermore, these regulations often prevented some whites from voting. Because some whites were in fact disfranchised, it is possible that Bourbon Democrats of the late nineteenth century deliberately framed laws designed to eliminate poor white voters, who opposed the planter- and industry-oriented Bourbon faction of the Democratic party. Evidence indicates that the blacks who voted in the South after Reconstruction usually supported the conservative officeholders, and restrictions on all blacks would have cut into this sector of the Bourbons' voter base. Documentation is slim, but there appears to be some truth in the charge that Bourbons wrote laws with loopholes so that some blacks could vote and some whites could not. While Bourbon racism was strong, it was not strong enough to prevent the Bourbons from doing whatever seemed necessary to remain in office.

A more informal yet more effective way of limiting black voters than any of the previous methods was the so-called white primary. Wisconsin is generally credited with having first used the direct primary system in 1903, but in fact South Carolina established one in 1896, and a majority of southern states were already using it when Wisconsin adopted its system. By 1915 the remaining states in the region had instituted direct primaries. Since primary elections were more important than general elections in states where one party prevailed, party leaders in the southern states drew up rules for voting in the Democratic primaries that effectively disfranchised many black voters. In the South the direct primary meant a white primary, and it was no surprise that the South strongly supported the national Progressive movement's drive for a direct primary system.

Because the Constitution prohibits discrimination by the states on the basis of race, the white primary provided a means by which a black could be prevented from voting without disturbing legally oriented white southern minds. The Democratic party dominated politics in the southern states, but that did not mean that the party and the state government were legally synonymous. If the party, acting as a purely private organization, prescribed rules that excluded blacks from voting in the primary, in no way could a state violate the Fifteenth Amendment. That the Democratic primary was in effect the only election in southern states did not trouble southern consciences; indeed, southerners were content with an arrangement that disfranchised the black man, yet did not violate the letter of the Constitution. In the years before the First World War most white primary arrangements were quite informal. Some states promulgated party rules designed to be used throughout the state, other states gave local or county party leaders discretion regarding black voters in the primaries, and in other instances state and local election committees simply refused to permit blacks to be handed ballots for primary elections in the absence of any state party rule on the subject. Except for a few metropolitan areas such as Memphis and San Antonio, the white primary eventually prevailed in the entire South.

Historically, southern conservative politicians had a tradition of race baiting; therefore, it was no surprise when their racism surfaced. The seemingly paradoxical racism of the Progressives was more difficult to understand. How could Progressives reconcile their words and actions in regard to the black man with their interest in human welfare and in increased political democracy? Were not the Progressives inconsistent and really not "progressive," since they were insensitive to the rights and feelings of the black man? For some the answer to the latter question was yes; they were mainly interested in attaining office for themselves, and without conscience they played upon white fears of blacks in their campaigns, while in office their primary efforts were to hold down the black man. They knew they seemed philosophically inconsistent, but that was unimportant as long as they could be elected. The majority of the Progressives, however, saw no paradox, no inconsistency; rather they looked upon the control of the black man as a vital part of Progressive reform. When the great majority of whites believed that blacks were innately inferior, it was logical, reasonable, and desirable to proscribe black political activity. When Progressives called for more political democracy, they meant eliminating the "ignorant and vicious" elements of the electorate. They wanted to "purify the electorate," and the primary goal of that purification was the exclusion of black voters.

Governor Montague of Virginia shared the feelings of his fellow Progressives. He believed that most blacks had neither the intelligence nor the character to vote. He wrote: "The foundation of Republican government . . . consists in the virtue and intelligence of its electorate. Either dishonesty or ignorance is fatal to free institutions." Having seen the Bourbons buy black votes wholesale, Montague concluded that it would be better to disfranchise blacks than to have them involved in the voting process unintelligently or used as a pawn by white men. Montague would disfranchise the purchasable black, rescuing the suffrage from its odium of illiteracy and barter. He concluded that elections would thus be rid of undemocratic elements; opportunities for political maneuver by machine politicians would be restricted; the need for Democratic solidarity would be destroyed; and a two-party system would emerge. The South would then manifest the kind of democratic politics worthy of a Progressive region. Furthermore, disfranchisement would bury the issue of white supremacy, and the white populace could view other political issues of the day with more objectivity. Montague did not see disfranchisement as permanent; he favored establishing educational qualifications for suffrage while providing blacks with adequate education. He concluded, "Eventually we may expect the development of a negro electorate determined upon sound political principles." Unlike some other Progressives, Montague did not appeal to white voters by denouncing blacks, except in regard to the franchise. He held typical southern attitudes about the inferiority of the black socially, culturally, and intellectually; but as governor he publicly condemned lynching and he once sent troops to protect a black man who was in danger of being lynched. Montague saw no inconsistency in his attitudes and actions, and he would have been offended had he been criticized for holding Progressive and racist views simultaneously.

Other southern Progressives agreed in principle with Montague's views, even though they did not often spell them out so precisely and systematically. While advocating reforms in regard to education, liquor, child labor, trusts, and the like, they naturally extended their reforming efforts to the electorate. Black disfranchisement, therefore, rather than being at odds with progressivism, reflected the unique spirit of the southern Progressive movement.

THE SOUTH AND THE NATION

Fifty-three different men were elected to the twenty-two southern seats in the Senate from 1900 to 1917. Except for North Carolina's Populist Marion Butler, who left the Senate in March 1901, and Republican Jeter C. Pritchard, who had been elected by Tarheel voters on a Populist-Republican "cooperationist" ticket and whose term expired in 1903, all of these men were Democrats. The results of one-party politics were equally apparent in the southern delegations to the House of Representatives. The southern states filled approximately one hundred seats in each Congress from 1900 to 1917, and Democrats occupied ninety-three to ninety-six of these. Tennessee usually had two Republicans·in its ten-man delegation, and depending upon the Congress, North Carolina had from one to three Republicans and Virginia one in their delegations of ten. At the beginning of the twentieth century Alabama had one Republican legislator, and during the next dozen years Texas occasionally sent a GOP member to Congress. The other southern delegations were solidly Democratic.

A study of the fifty-three senators from southern states reveals several general characteristics. A significant proportion were Civil War veterans, usually common soldiers or lesser officers. The majority began their political careers during the Bourbon era, and except for one or two, all had been active Bourbon Democrats. They had often served in the state legislature, and more than a few had been governors of their states before being elected to the Senate. By then many were in their declining years; nine died between 1900 and 1917 while still in office. After having served the Democratic party in their respective states, these southerners had often been elevated to the Senate not because they were expected to make large contributions at the national level, but rather because they deserved the honor. A Senate seat was regarded as a sinecure, a paid position of prestige with little or no responsibility and few requirements of active service. These senators looked after their constituents' interests, threw their political weight around in their home states, and occasionally made comments about blacks and foreign affairs on the floor of the Senate. Under the circumstances, it is not surprising that they were out of step with Progressive ideas of the time.

Despite their generally conservative bent, however, a few of the old-line southern senators responded favorably to specific reforms. Two or three strayed from Bourbon policies when they voted to regulate the railroads, and one worked hard to protect the nation's forests from lumbering interests. Another favored the establishment of a corporation commission and spoke out for larger protection of labor interests. Favoring a specific reform or two did not make these men Progressives; their policies simply happened to coincide with northern Progressive ideas. On most issues they stolidly defended the status quo.

Senators James P. Clarke and Jeff Davis of Arkansas, Benjamin Tillman and Ellison D. ("Cotton Ed") Smith of South Carolina, and Joseph W. Bailey of Texas may be labeled as partial Progressives. During the presidencies of Theodore Roosevelt and William Howard Taft, one or all of these five senators favored stronger railroad regulation, antitrust laws, bills to prohibit the sale of intoxicating liquors in Prohibition territory, legislation to regulate Wall Street and speculators, lower tariffs, the Sixteenth and Seventeenth Amendments to the Constitution, and a reorganization of the currency and banking system. Even though they were not full-fledged Progressives, their presence in Washington revealed a modicum of southern progressivism on the national scene.

Approximately twenty-five out of the hundred-odd southern congressmen in any given Congress revealed more than passing Progressive tendencies. Their influence should not be overemphasized, but they did play an active role in the development of Progressive legislation. Insurgent Republicans and southern Progressives formed a formidable coalition. The southerners supported and in some instances initiated measures such as the Hepburn Act (which Mississippi Senator John Sharp Williams claimed to have fathered), the Mann-Elkins Railroad Act, the pure food law, the meat inspection bill, the income tax amendment, tariff reductions, changes in the House rules that curtailed the Speaker's powers (and thus reduced the powers of "the interests"), the amendment establishing direct election of U.S. senators, a bill providing publicity for campaign expenditures before elections, the Canadian reciprocity bill, the children's bureau bill, the postal savings measure, the parcel post law, and over twenty labor laws (including those for an eight-hour day, an anti-injunction bill, a workmen's compensation bill, an employer's liability bill, and an act to limit the hours of railroad employees engaged in interstate commerce). They were in the forefront on the joint resolution to approve the constitutions of Arizona and New Mexico, since they liked the provisions for the initiative, referendum, and recall in the Arizona document. They also aided major congressional investigations into steel, sugar, and money trusts.

Support for these measures exposed as myth the idea that only die-hard conservatives represented the South, and a fair analysis of southern political behavior in Washington in the Roosevelt-Taft period undermines the concept that the region was politically solid. The makeup of the congressional delegations revealed a growing bifactionalism that was soon to be the hallmark of politics in many southern states.

The influence of southerners in Washington, including a growing group of Progressives, increased after Woodrow Wilson became president in 1913. Democrats controlled both houses of Congress for the first time since 1894, and long-tenured southerners were elevated to positions of influence as chairmen of most of the important standing committees. Clarke of Arkansas was elected president pro tempore of the Senate in 1913, and Thomas S. Martin of Virginia became Senate majority leader in 1917. Southerners were chairmen of all major Senate committees except those on agriculture, banking and currency, and interstate commerce; moreover, they chaired a disproportionately large number of minor Senate committees. In the House the Democratic majority leader was Oscar W. Underwood of Alabama, who in 1915 was replaced by North Carolina's Claude Kitchin. The chairmanship roster of the major House committees in 1913 included eight southerners. Since Democrats controlled both Congress and the presidency for the first time in nearly two decades, Democratic hopes for the implementation of their programs ran high; with a native southerner in the White House and with numerous southerners influential in Congress, southern hopes soared even higher.

In the presidential campaign of 1912 Woodrow Wilson espoused a political theory he labeled the "New Freedom." Basically a states' rights Jeffersonian, Wilson feared the power of a large central government; he believed that the government's role was to abolish special privileges and artificial barriers preventing the development of individual energies and to guarantee free and fair competition in the business world. He believed that the most important question facing the American people was the preservation of their economic freedom. When competition was unregu-

lated, monopoly developed; honest competition could flourish
only if the trusts were broken up. In speech after speech, Wilson
had stated that the main task of the next president was to provide
the means to free business from the chains of monopoly and
special privilege. As the campaign progressed Wilson came to
believe that he was battling for the old American way of life; he
was convinced that economic democracy was absolutely essential
to political democracy. Such views gave ultimate meaning to his
campaign slogan.

Once elected, Wilson strove to implement his New Freedom
principles through a series of laws passed by Congress. Both
conservative and Progressive southern senators and congressmen
supported these efforts to lower the tariff, reorganize the nation's
banking system, expand the currency, and regulate the trusts. But
they directed more of their attention to matters of specific concern
to their constituencies, including agricultural reform. Since the
mid-nineteenth century a movement to improve agricultural
conditions through rural credit reform had been in existence.
During the first decade of the twentieth century, objective
observers acknowledged that the commercial banking system on
which the farmer depended was not adapted to his needs, that the
financial machinery used by other classes of borrowers was
inadequate for the farmer, and that the farmer's rate of interest
was higher than what railroads, municipalities, or industrial
corporations paid. All three political parties had endorsed rural
credit in their national conventions of 1912, and President Wilson
had expressed the need for reform in this field in his inaugural
address. Florida's Senator Duncan U. Fletcher wrote and introduced a bill to establish a system of privately controlled land
banks to operate under federal charter. A provision of the bill
required the government to furnish capital for the land banks and
to buy their bonds if private investors failed to do so. This
measure, called the Hollis-Bulkley bill, set off a controversy when
the clause stipulating government support was made public.
President Wilson and Secretary of Agriculture David F. Houston
held that this would be special legislation for a particular group
and not in the tradition of New Freedom principles. The
spokesmen for the bill disagreed; they were convinced that in the
farmers' attempt to gain independence from private bankers a
rural credit system without governmental support and sponsorship
could never succeed. When House agrarian leaders proceeded to
introduce the bill despite Wilson's opposition, the president hinted

that he would veto it if the "radical propositions" were included. This development angered southern agrarian leaders, but they yielded to the pressure and temporarily halted their agitation for rural credit.

Agrarian leaders in 1916 passed the Federal Farm Loan Act, guided through the Senate by Thomas P. Gore of Oklahoma and the House by Asbury F. Lever of South Carolina, chairmen of the respective agriculture committees. Despite his earlier misgivings, the president signed the bill, which established a system composed of twelve federal farm loan banks capitalized at $500,000 each, whose essential function was to provide credit for farmers at a low rate of interest on a long-term basis. This act, called the "Magna Carta of American farm finance," was a distinct victory for southern agrarian leaders and represented their major achievement during Wilson's first administration.

Southern agrarian Democrats had less difficulty enacting the Smith-Lever Act of 1914 and the Smith-Hughes Act of 1917. The first, sponsored by Lever in the House and Hoke Smith in the Senate, created a generous grant-in-aid system in behalf of agricultural education through university and governmental extension work in farm villages. Sponsored by two Georgians, Smith and Representative Dudley M. Hughes, the Smith-Hughes Act created a federal board for vocational education to administer a grant-in-aid system that generously subsidized state efforts in the teaching of commercial, industrial, agricultural, and domestic arts.

Representing rural constituencies, southern senators and congressmen had always devoted time and energy to legislation designed to help the farmer and farming. During the Wilson era, when attention focused on the status of the "little man," all southern legislators forcefully directed attention to the conditions of southern farmers. Whether Progressive or conservative, the southern agrarian leaders took advantage of the Progressive climate to agitate for beneficial farm legislation. Conservatives who did not generally favor federal government action at the local level were not embarrassed to call for farm supports; Progressives were pleased that their principles were in agreement with their public postures in the interests of the folks back home. By happy coincidence southern legislators were able to advocate and obtain legislation for their constituencies while Congress and the nation were in the mood for compliance. The farm legislation of the Wilson years reflected the power of the southern delegations in Washington.

The Farmers' Answer

A poster on Prohibition, a national crusade that found support among southern farmers and Progressives. (Courtesy of the Library of Congress)

When the Wilson administration began in 1913, knowledgeable observers had predicted that the new president would have the most difficulty with conservative southern Democrats as he attempted to move New Freedom legislation through Congress while he and the southern Progressives would get along famously. The prophets were not very accurate. The president made a point of conferring with the recognized leaders in Congress, and on the whole his approach was quite successful as he worked closely with southern conservatives such as Underwood, Furnifold M. Simmons, and Carter Glass. Wilson and the Progressives were not always at odds, but more friction developed between them than between the president and the conservatives. The Progressives pushed and tugged Wilson further to the left than he would have preferred to go, but in the end he was happy with the legislation they produced.

When northern Progressives pushed for enactment of a group of so-called social justice measures, southerners in Washington generally expressed opposition. Even though southern Progressives had contributed significantly to the enlargement of the government's responsibilities by favoring more federal control over the tariff, the trusts, banking, and business, they often balked when asked to extend their Progressive ideas into the realm of human relationships. Although they had been in the vanguard in the drive for rural credit, which by any description must be called a fight for social justice, as a group they joined their conservative colleagues to oppose advancement for women, immigrants, and blacks, primarily because of their racial fears. They opposed an amendment to the Constitution that would permit women to vote, taking the public position that only the states had the constitutional power to extend suffrage. Privately they admitted that their opposition stemmed mainly from their fear that if such an amendment were passed, it might lead to *black* women voting— and to this they were ardently opposed. They viewed immigrants as competition for native-born American laborers and as depressors of wages; therefore, they favored imposing restrictions on immigration to the United States. Like southern local and state leaders, the South's politicians in Washington hoped to proscribe black Americans' activities. During Wilson's first term, they introduced into Congress over two dozen antiblack measures, "the greatest flood of bills proposing discriminatory legislation against Negroes" ever to come before the national legislature. Many of these proposals related to blacks living in the nation's capital. In

1913, after five minutes of debate, the House passed an antimiscegenation bill for the District of Columbia, but Senate inaction killed it. Southerners advanced proposals for residential restrictions in Washington, and they introduced no fewer than four bills to establish Jim Crow streetcars there. The House Committee on the District of Columbia reported one of the latter bills in February 1915, but it died in the House. Such proposals were direct slaps at the center of black society in the United States. In the last census Washington had counted 94,446 blacks in its population; transportational and residential segregation would have denied black Washingtonians the modicum of equality in certain areas of life they already enjoyed.

Other bills were directed toward American blacks generally, such as a suggestion for civil service segregation. Mississippi's Vardaman had been elected to the Senate in 1911 on a platform demanding modification of the Fourteenth Amendment and the repeal of the Fifteenth, and after Wilson's election he dropped such proposals into the Senate hopper. In January 1915 the House passed a bill making marriage illegal between white persons and persons with one-eighth or more "Negro blood," but the Senate never considered the bill. At a time when many states were enacting discriminatory legislation, southern representatives were making some attempts to do the same in Congress. They were unsuccessful, but these few attempts and the absence of positive legislation for blacks revealed a southern-dominated Congress that had little conscience for social justice, at least in regard to race; social justice was to be for whites only.

In many ways the Wilson administration had more effect upon southern state and local politics than southern politicians in Washington had upon national legislation. The first southern-born president since Andrew Johnson, Wilson both reflected and contributed to southern progressivism. Powerful beyond their numbers, southern Progressives had much to do with Wilson's nomination in 1912, and they were in the vanguard of the campaign against the Republicans in the general election. The Wilson movement in the South was a fundamental struggle for "progressive Democracy," and aroused a great deal of interest in popular government and Progressive reform. Southern Progressives who had been thwarted at the state level supported the Wilson movement, thereby gaining something of a national base while promoting the development of bifactional politics in their region. Moreover, southerners were proud of the fact that, after so long a drought, someone from their region again resided in the White House.

Despite Wilson's willingness to support the enactment of a major part of the Progressive program, however, the new president disappointed his loyal followers in the South. While he and most of the newer southern leaders held similarly moderate Progressive principles, the president was compelled to work for party unity. Whatever his principles, he could not afford to offend powerful congressional leaders and committee chairmen from the South, many of whom were quite conservative. He had to consider their stands and possible opposition as he attempted to implement his moderate program. This political maneuvering on the president's part caused him to conflict occasionally with southern Progressives in Congress, but more importantly it caused Progressive state leaders to feel slighted, since they had hoped the national administration would support their attempts to overthrow conservative opponents at the state level. Progressives protested Wilson's patronage policies that strengthened the control of the conservative factions, but in vain.

Southern Progressives were also unhappy when the Wilsonian program was watered down as a result of pressure from the South's industrial promoters. By the time Wilson was elected president, the trend toward industrialization in the South had been so strong that industrial leaders had the numbers and power to influence southern politicians. The textile mill owners in the Carolinas and Georgia, the iron and steel manufacturers in Alabama, and the railroad companies in every southern state took unequivocal positions on legislation dealing with banking and currency, the tariff, trusts, and child labor. Mindful of these economic interests and the political leaders who spoke in their behalf, Wilson often disappointed his more ardent southern supporters.

Yet Wilson was a strong president who aroused southerners' interest in national affairs, and by so doing he pulled southern politicians into the orbit of national politics. Local and state leaders in the South were attracted to Wilsonian liberalism, and they came to realize during the Wilson era that only the national government was capable of solving some of their states' problems. The long-range implications of that recognition would someday help to lessen the South's affinity for states' rights.

Progressivism was an influential factor in the South from the turn of the century to the time of American entrance into the world war. The Progressive movement was not a fad or momentary diversion in the life of the South but rather bore seriously upon the developments in the region. The South long had had a feeling of togetherness, perhaps more so than any other region of the country; and it was only natural for southerners occasionally to take stock of their region's needs and attempt to work together to fulfill them. The Progressive movement clearly suited southern susceptibilities and traditions at that time.

Nor could there be any question of the racism that filled the columns of southern newspapers during the Progressive era. Racism was a product of the times, not merely in the South or in the United States but in western Europe as well. Southern racism was not extraordinary in its appearances and manifestations, but it was more notable, more open and violent, than racial feelings elsewhere.

As for the third aspect of southern life during the Progressive era, the South's participation in national politics, the years between 1901 and 1917 saw not merely the triumph of the Democratic party in the presidential election of 1912 and again in the election of 1916, but the triumph of southern congressmen in the organization of the House and Senate. After the debacle of the Civil War and the long decades of near political oblivion, after the slow evaporation of the deep suspicion of southerners that filled northerners and westerners for years, the appearance of Wilson in the White House supplied the South with an opportunity to reach the highest positions in the federal government, and in that sense the Wilson administration marked the return of the South to political power and paved the way for southern participation in national affairs.

TWO

The First
World War
and Its
Aftermath The Progressive movement in
the years after the turn of the
century demonstrated that the South had become part of
the nation, that any large development of ideas and action in the
country was bound to affect that region as well. It was only
natural, then, that when the first southern-born president since
just after the Civil War, Woodrow Wilson, asked for a declaration
of war against Imperial Germany in April 1917, the South like the
rest of the nation found new requirements placed upon its ways of
life and livelihood. The war vastly stimulated the region's
economy. Cotton had many wartime uses. The South's mild
climate together with availability of cheap building materials
dictated that many of the huge new army camps should be built
south of the Mason-Dixon line. Moreover, the economic opportunities of the war drove many southerners, whites as well as blacks,
toward the industrial cities of the North where good jobs were

waiting. Once southerners began to move out of the region, even if
(so many of them thought) temporarily, they raised their expectations of what the good life should be; they either stayed or took
their revised expectations back to their own region. In the case of
the blacks, the movement northward resulted in a new way of life.
Many of them never returned, and there commenced a rapid
change in the population of the North's cities that would soon
rearrange innumerable aspects of American life.

Southern politics during the postwar years necessarily
reflected wartime experiences. The factionalism within the Democratic party that had emerged during the Progressive era was
muffled during the year and a half of the war, 1917–18, when
American troops were fighting in France; unity was the watch-
word. But in the postwar years, down to the Great Crash in 1929,
intraparty battles reappeared. A modified form of progressivism
developed during the twenties, in the South as well as elsewhere in
the nation. The strong religious strain in southern life asserted
itself in politics in interesting ways. Racism continued, but the war
had given opportunities to blacks which inspired black leaders to
ask for more freedom, not merely economic but personal. The war
and its aftermath thus marked the second major twentieth-century
force upon southern politics, progressivism being the first. Any
observer of the South could sense the quickening pace of change.

WAR AND POLITICS

The First World War wrought major political changes in the
South. After Reconstruction the county had gradually become
central to local government and politics. Self-perpetuating oligar-
chies, usually composed of land-rich planters, had dominated
local government in the antebellum South, but during the
Bourbon ascendancy the political center of gravity, following the
shift of economic power, moved from the countryside to the
county seats. Well before 1900, local merchants, small businessmen, and lawyers had replaced the planters as the governing class.
At the same time the South as a region was withdrawing from the
national political scene, state and local politics turned inward.
When these cliques of new politicians became dominant in local
politics, "courthouse rings" developed in most of the more than
fifteen hundred counties in the southern states. By the time of the
First World War, "politics" was virtually synonymous with
"courthouse politics" in the South, and a self-satisfied "Main

Street crowd" for years controlled political offices, consolidated economic power, and enjoyed social prestige. If laws prohibited serving more than one or two terms as county treasurer, in the next election the officer ran for county sheriff or court clerk. Some petty officeholders spent a lifetime rotating from one county position to another. In a region dominated by one-party politics, party affiliation was not an issue as voters continued to elect these local leaders to office. The repair of county roads, the rate of local taxation, and the question of who would fill a few county-controlled jobs were often the major concerns of the voters, and the local politicians did not attempt to expand their horizons.

The county seat politicians were generally conservative in political and social outlook, viewing with suspicion social change and liberal concepts. Getting ahead in business and the professions, making money, and enjoying the benefits of material possessions were often their personal goals. Though these new leaders believed in the doctrine of hard work, they did not hesitate to use economic or political "pull" for their own benefit. The county seat leader was usually suspicious of intellectuals, and his creed was allegiance to God, the United States, and democracy. Offering lip service to the democratic credo of liberty, equality, and majority rule, he did not extend these concepts to include Republicans or people with black skins. In these respects the new politicians differed little from the former rulers, the planter aristocracy; one political scientist has observed that the ghost of the antebellum landed gentry hovered over Cottonton, Millville, and Tobaccoburg.

During this period when southern states concentrated on economic problems and when they were little involved in national politics, many southern state leaders reflected the attitudes of the county politicians. In the 1890s Tillman promised that if South Carolinians sent him to Washington, he would stick a pitchfork into the fat ribs of President Grover Cleveland; but few other politicians talked to the voters about national politics, and even Tillman's reference was prompted primarily by his belief that the government in Washington was not responsive to southern needs. Political interest in the South was regional and local, not national. The national government seldom acted in a way that would affect state and local politics, and southern politicians and their constituencies did not look to Washington for solutions to their problems. They ignored the national scene not only because of their overwhelming devotion to local issues, but also because their commitment to states' rights was developing into an ideological revulsion against national interference in state affairs—especially as the national government became more powerful. This principle was soon to become a major article of faith.

Whatever their limited views or their narrow political focus, state and local leaders advocated increased economic development for the South. These men matched the efforts of the Bourbons to attract business and industry. On behalf of "progress," they unabashedly contacted industrial decision makers in their attempts to entice industry to their little urban centers. No event more directly speeded up these politicians' interest in regional economic development than the outbreak of the First World War. Sensing the economic impact of a wartime economy on their region, county seat politicians extolled the advantages and opportunities of their areas for the location of industrial plants and government facilities of all kinds. State leaders, many of whom had never been outside their states, traveled to Washington to lobby at a higher level, and southerners who had been elected to serve in Washington used their offices to bring the fruits of a wartime economy to their native area. The war enticed state and local politicians out of their narrow boundaries, though their concerns remained essentially self-serving. The politicians' industry-hunting forays impressed the southern electorate, especially when southerners directly profited from the presence of a new industrial plant in their locality. Voters, observing the economic impact of a new industry, began to demand that political aspirants take a positive stand on the subject of industrial development, and the politicians happily obliged with promises they sincerely tried to fulfill. Southern politics and economic development were more than ever securely tied together.

When war began in 1914, southerners showed immediate concern for the effect hostilities might have on the cotton trade, so dependent upon the unregulated world market. Soon after the turn of the century, after years of marginal existence, southern cotton farmers had begun to make money, primarily because of rising demand for raw cotton resulting in higher prices. On the eve of the war cotton was selling for thirteen cents a pound, and in the fields at the time a large crop of over sixteen million bales was ripening for harvest. But the farmers' fears of the impact of the war were justified; as soon as it broke out cotton prices fell sharply. When the major cotton exchanges did not open on 3 August and when they remained closed for three months, the southerners recognized that the crop then in the fields faced ruin unless something could be done quickly. The South's agricultural spokesmen advanced all the panaceas that had been suggested in past cotton crises, including crop diversification, crop limitation, more adequate credit arrangements, and federal storage facilities for cotton while growers waited to sell at more favorable prices. Most of these suggestions were rejected and many of them would not have been effective anyway.

Although southern agrarian leaders believed in states' rights and had in the recent past opposed the federal government's intrusion into areas they considered properly within the states' domain, the condition of cotton was desperate. Like their constituents, the politicians overlooked principles in view of the importance of cotton to the southern economy. These leaders hoped that the federal government would find relief for the cotton South, but they were disappointed. After a conference of southern farm leaders, businessmen, and politicians in late August, the suggestion was made that the government purchase surplus cotton at a predetermined price. This idea was rejected out of hand, Treasury Secretary William McAdoo calling it one of those "perfectly wild and ridiculous schemes." The Wilson administration opposed other plans offered in Congress because they catered too much to "special privilege" and were not in keeping with New Freedom principles. Southerners who had earlier hoped to dominate the Wilson administration found that once again the president was not responsive to their demands. Fortunately, the South's problem was solved when British firms began to buy more cotton, stabilizing the price of the South's money crop and relieving the need for government supports.

Of considerable concern to southern leaders in Washington was the British blockade of German ports, even though cotton was not originally listed as contraband of war. When the British government decided to place cotton on the contraband list, British leaders realized that they were unwise to antagonize the South; they worked to soften the blow to that region by encouraging British textile mills to purchase larger quantities of cotton. Southern leaders in Washington still denounced the ban on cotton, but as the months passed and the price of cotton rose, the South's anger and anti-British feeling subsided.

Most southern senators and congressmen supported President Wilson's defense and preparedness program. They backed Wilson because of their loyalty to the Democratic party, because they trusted the southern-born president, and because they believed in a strong national defensive posture. But a vocal minority of southerners in the Progressive-pacifist tradition criticized military preparations; they noted that preparedness measures directed attention away from Progressive legislation and they feared that a military buildup might lead the nation into war. The critics made little impression upon their constituencies, however; the majority of the southern populace supported by words or at least silence the nation's military preparations.

When the United States entered the war, the Wilson administration made determined efforts to cultivate the American people's support of the war effort, and southerners no less than northerners responded positively to the patriotic appeals. In Congress southerners supported legislation designed to help win the war. On eight major war measures—conscription, the Espionage Act, the Sedition Act, the Lever Food Control Act, the Railroad Act of 1918, the Overman Act, and antifilibuster resolutions in 1917 and 1918—southern congressmen and senators cast only twenty-one negative votes. Since these acts granted broad powers to the national government, southern abandonment of states' rights during the wartime emergency was nothing short of phenomenal.

A vocal minority expressed opposition to war measures, however. Senator Thomas Hardwick of Georgia, Congressman Kitchin, and Senator Vardaman were among the southern opponents of Wilson's policies. Although they varied in their intensity and opposition to specific measures, these critics particularly disliked conscription, food control, and the espionage bills. They believed that the conscription and espionage laws infringed upon individual liberties, and they reasoned that the food control bill violated states' rights. While these southern dissenters embarrassed the nation and the administration throughout the war, they were ineffective in their opposition and received little public support.

Southern war opponents were successful only in taxing war profits and corporate wealth to help pay for the costly war. These southern Democrats were mainly responsible for reducing certain tax exemptions and raising tax rates generally by means of the war revenue acts of 1917 and 1918. Congress also passed surtaxes, increased inheritance taxes, and established higher levies on excess profits because of the pressure from these men. In this area the dissenters were not out of step with their constituents. Rural southerners strongly distrusted the great financial interests and they believed that munitions manufacturers wanted war in order to increase profits. Blease invariably got a round of applause from South Carolina audiences when he repeatedly stated that "if it hadn't been for money interests in England, we wouldn't be in the war." Not surprisingly, many poor rural southerners sided with Kitchin and Vardaman in their demands for higher levies on war profits. "Who will pay the taxes?" Kitchin asked. "Wealth, and not poverty," he answered, and poverty-ridden southern farmers agreed with him. But among southerners at large fear of profiteering was less important than winning the war, and they continued to support the president rather than his critics.

The fate of the president's detractors in their next political campaigns is indicative of southern response to Wilson's management of the war. The Democratic primaries of 1918 spelled disaster for most of those who had opposed Wilson's policies. In Texas's Seventh District, Jeff McLemore, who had disagreed with Wilson's policy of neutrality at the beginning of the war, failed to win a majority in any county. Of the five southern congressmen who voted against war with Germany, only two were reelected. Senators Vardaman and Hardwick were both defeated for renomination, neither ever managing a political comeback after these reversals. Blease and Watson of Georgia attempted to reenter politics in that year, but Blease failed in a bid for a Senate seat and Wilson-critic Watson lost in a race for the House.

The purge of anti-Wilson Democrats had not been wholly successful, but it was effective enough to still most dissident southern voices, and southern support of the administration's policies continued in peacetime until the end of the Wilsonian era. In the Senate debates on the Treaty of Versailles and United States membership in the League of Nations, southern Democrats overwhelmingly supported Wilsonian leadership. Even after it became obvious that the Senate could not pass the unamended treaty demanded by Wilson, the president's southern followers remained faithful to their uncompromising leader. Republicans, northern Democrats, and the president shared responsibility for the defeat of the treaty, but in the final analysis the majority of the southern Democrats, by taking a strong partisan stand, were the most significant element in the disaster. The South's role in rejecting United States membership in the League of Nations revealed power misplaced in the first real excursion of southern politicians into the international arena since before the Civil War.

The majority of the local, state, and national southern

politicians were generally pleased with the effects of the First World War in their region. After the end of the cotton crisis of 1914, southerners discovered that the nation and the world were in need of the goods they produced. More money from southern cash crops found its way into southern farmers' pockets than in any previous four years within memory. Mortgages were reduced, improvements were made on farm buildings and fences, and new machinery replaced aging and often-repaired relics. Southern officeholders claimed credit for economic solvency, and voters returned them to office at the next election; dissatisfaction normally expressed in the voting booth was virtually nonexistent. The developing courthouse rings were more firmly entrenched, governors were reelected, and senators and congressmen gained additional tenure in Washington. Democrats in the nation's capital were to return to a minority status at the end of the war, but southerners increased their power within the party when Democratic strength in other parts of the country declined.

The war had forced southerners to permit national and international concerns to share the stage formerly dominated by provincial politics; the all-important cotton crop was seriously endangered by the war's effects on the international market. The South's commitment to states' rights was shaken by an emergency demanding a powerful central government. Southern politicians expressed their unhappiness with growing national power, but they did not discourage federal expenditures in their region—a contradictory position that was soon to become a tradition in southern politics.

ECONOMICS AND SOCIETY

The industrial boom in the South during the First World War did not abate in the postwar decade. Textile mills continued to produce mountains of goods, and promoters scurried around the Piedmont to interest more localities in supporting new mills. Gaston County, North Carolina, adopted the slogan "Organize a mill a week." This magnificent dream was not fulfilled, but by 1929 the county was the leading textile producer in the South, third in the entire nation. Statistics for the first three years of the twenties showed that nearly a thousand mills were constructed or expanded, and each succeeding year of the decade saw the South's textile industry activate more spindles, produce more cloth, and pay out more wages. The South's tobacco industry grew primarily as the result of the cigarette revolution and the fierce competition between the Duke empire and newcomer Robert H. Reynolds. In 1930 the South produced 125 billion cigarettes, a more than 1,000 percent increase in twenty years. Industrial expansion was also great in the lumber, railroad, metal, chemical, and oil industries.

Southern progressivism had been dormant during the war years, but it surfaced in the form of "business progressivism" in the postwar decade. Devotion to the South's material progress was the prime characteristic of this revived reform movement. Unlike their prewar predecessors, the "business progressives" did not attempt to root out the trusts and entrenched "privilege"; rather economic conditions in the South at the beginning of the 1920s caused many politicians to be proindustry. They recognized the benefits of industrial expansion and encouraged it. Southern governors established industrial commissions, made personal forays into the North and Europe to lure industries or investors to the South, dangled tax advantages before prospective companies, and freely advertised the southern industrial capabilities. In addition to advocating industrial progress, the postwar business progressives favored efficient government and expanded public services, the latter including education and good roads. "Progressive" states and communities were those that had economical governments, better schools, sound businesses, and thriving industrial plants.

While running for office many southern governors talked about "good government," implying that they favored economic retrenchment, tax reform, and the reduction of state salaries; but the administrations of these business progressives revealed that they really desired to reduce waste and corruption rather than cut back public services. When these postwar Progressives were safely in office, they raised the salaries of underpaid state employees, instituted executive budget systems, and established central purchasing offices or other sound policies to insure the wise expenditure of state funds. Between 1918 and 1929 every southern state had installed a budget system, most of them had adopted general reorganization plans, and almost every state inaugurated administrative and tax reforms. Whenever the politicians pledged themselves to tax reform, they usually meant more equitable taxation, not a reduction in taxes. Indeed, most states spent more money than they took in during the decade, and whatever they said about penny-wise spending, they approved state action increasing expenditures for public health services, prison reform, hospitals, charitable institutions, and child welfare.

The prewar beginnings of public health services were considerably expanded in the postwar decade. In some cases political leaders led fights to eradicate hookworm, malaria, tuberculosis, and pellagra, diseases that had felled an untold number of southerners in past decades. Certainly state boards of health could not have operated without financial support from state treasuries. To educate southerners to wear shoes, to screen their homes, to eat fresh vegetables, and to improve the sanitary conditions of their surroundings was no small task. It was by no means completed in the decade of the twenties, but public health officials and state and local political leaders combined forces to make significant headway. Public health services did not attract as much attention and money as education, but they received a fair share of the states' revenues.

The politicians were most responsive to the South's greatest challenge, education. Much had been done to overcome the region's massive illiteracy in the first two decades of the twentieth century, but the battle was far from over. Except in the South's larger cities, the high school was still in its infancy in 1920, and widely dispersed one-room schools with poorly trained teachers were the rule. The school consolidation movement was in its incipient stages, delayed until hard-surfaced roads would permit school buses to travel long distances to carry children to larger and better educational facilities. School buildings were often in bad repair and school supplies and aids were scarce or nonexistent. North Carolina had a succession of governors in the 1920s who poured state income into impoverished schools; by the end of the decade the state had outdistanced its neighbors in educational development. Governors in other states made some progress in inaugurating minimum school terms (usually six months in length), increasing public school financing, upgrading teacher training programs, and founding colleges. In 1930 every southern state still lagged behind northern states in average expenditure per pupil, but during the preceding decade eight southern states had exceeded the national rate of increase. In 1921 South Carolina had the lowest public school expenditure in the nation; by 1929 it had the highest rate of increase. The work of philanthropic foundations and the unending efforts of dedicated educational leaders were important factors in the region's educational advance, aided by southern governors and their legislatures who were willing to appropriate money to state departments of education.

The newly created state highway departments were often among the largest consumers of state funds. As southern governors traveled around their states, they realized the validity of farmers' complaints about inadequate farm-to-market roads. Political and industrial leaders perceived that their drives to attract factories and mills to the South were useless unless the region had good roads to permit easy transportation of raw materials and finished products. The increased number of automobiles, mass-produced in Detroit and rushed to the South in large quantities, necessitated construction of improved roads; ribbons of dust and muddy quagmires in alternate seasons of the year were not conducive to the horseless carriage. Southern states set out to rectify sorry road conditions by building many miles of hard-surfaced roads costing millions of dollars. Arkansas's Governor John E. Martineau happily identified his administration with the slogan "Better roads and better schools," and Tennessee's Governor Austin Peay poured money into his good roads program. Early in the decade Virginia chose to build its roads as it collected gasoline and usage taxes to pay for them, but North Carolina voted a bond issue of $50 million to survey and build an interconnected system of improved roads. Tennessee followed North Carolina's lead even though economists predicted that such indebtedness was dangerous. In 1929 South Carolina voted a $65 million highway bond issue; the goal was to connect every county seat with an improved road. A major reason for southern acceptance of burdensome bond issues was that the national government had agreed to share the costs of constructing and maintaining interstate roads. The Federal Highway Act of 1921 resulted in the planning and constructing of an intersouthern highway system. Road financing by the national government abruptly ended a century-old political argument over federal aid for internal improvements. Muted were those southern voices that might have cried out against national support of the expanding interstate highways or against the sometimes strict supervision of the Federal Bureau of Highways. States' rights ideas were not applied to road financing; the practical benefits of good roads outweighed devotion to a constitutional principle.

Harry F. Byrd was a moderate whose administration espoused many of the cardinal tenets of the business progressivism of the twenties. After 1893 Virginia politics had been dominated by a machine put together by Thomas S. Martin and Claude A. Swanson. The organization and its new boss, Henry D. Flood, elected Byrd governor in 1925. While governor of Virginia from 1926 to 1930, he was concerned with efficiency in government and the promotion of industry. He believed that the administration of government should be efficiently conducted along the lines of well-organized business enterprises, although he recognized that the benefits of government could not be measured with a financial yardstick. As the cost of government increased, he saw the need of improved efficiency. He stressed that a state government should not extend beyond the discharge of functions that "public necessities have imposed on it" and that "undue extension" of governmental activities should be avoided. As governor, Byrd merged more than one hundred bureaus, boards, and commissions into fourteen departments. While he was launching a campaign to attract industry to the state, he was also battling oil companies for their alleged price discrimination, blocking telephone rate increases, and placing insurance rates under state control. In his early career he had revealed a penchant for careful spending by actively opposing a state bond issue for roads, but as governor he was swept along by the demand and desperate need for highways. His administration was responsible for increased taxes that made possible annual state expenditures of $14 million for highways, and by the end of his term he had given the state nearly five thousand miles of hard-surfaced roads.

A typical postwar business progressive was John M. Parker, the gentlemanly reformer who won the Louisiana governorship in 1920. Louisiana held a constitutional convention at the beginning of Parker's term, dealing with such politically explosive issues as income taxes, severance taxes, public roads, and education. The convention agreed that highway construction should proceed on a pay-as-you-go basis, and shortly thereafter the state legislature passed bills authorizing new construction. Before this time the parishes were mainly responsible for the construction and maintenance of roads; inadequate ones were the rule in the state, except in the wealthier parishes of Orleans, Caddo, and East Baton Rouge. Increased state aid for and supervision of public highway construction helped pull Louisianans from some of the deep mud bogs ironically called *high*ways. A two-cent gasoline tax and an annual tax on motor vehicles financed the construction program. In 1921 the state legislature created an appointive three-member highway commission, and within a half-dozen years Louisiana had provided for 162 "state highway routes," although most of these were not yet hard surfaced.

Parker advanced moderate proposals to tax the companies that were exploiting the state's natural resources. His sponsorship of a severance tax was a model of enlightened business progressivism; he used the money to expand Louisiana State University in lieu of raising state property taxes. Parker's conservationist tendencies were also evident when he ordered his attorney general to conduct an investigation of the carbon-black manufacturing plants that were wasting natural gas from the Monroe-Ouachita gas fields.

Louisiana's Huey P. Long, Jr., also embraced business progressivism; but he modified it, individualized it, and extended it to give Louisiana a radical program of positive economic and social reform, one of the most important ingredients of which was the personality of Huey himself. Long was a charismatic figure who knew how to relate both to the New Orleans populace and the poor voters in the rural areas of Louisiana. He knew when to clown and when not to, and he was not above caricaturing himself. He was an ambitious man—some thought dangerously so—and before his assassination in 1935 he had won national attention, compelling the president of the United States to take into consideration the force of his personality and power when recommending legislation to Congress and making important political decisions. Long has been referred to as a buffoon, a demagogue, a dictator, a Fascist, or a democrat, depending upon the frame of reference of the writer. T. Harry Williams, Long's most recent and thorough biographer, has said that the "Kingfish" was a mass leader who gave Louisianians what they wanted; this characteristic was the key to Long's ultimate success. In the hands of such a powerful and fascinating political personality, moderate business progressivism was molded beyond recognition.

In 1918 Long had successfully run for a post on the state railway commission (later the Public Service Commission). As a commissioner he had almost singlehandedly rolled back an increase in telephone rates, retroactive for two years, and he instantly became a state hero. He helped lower the rates of the Southwestern Gas and Electric Company, of Shreveport street-cars, and of all intrastate railroads, and he was a factor in the legislature's passage of a 3 percent severance tax on petroleum obtained from Louisiana wells.

In 1924 Long ran for the Louisiana governorship. He attacked the powerful Standard Oil Company, promised cheaper natural gas to New Orleans, good roads for everyone, free textbooks for all school children, and free trapping and fishing for all. He distributed thousands of circulars over the state, reprinting complimentary press editorials on the telephone rate reductions. He lost; but when he ran for governor in 1928 he renewed and enlarged his 1924 pledges, as he emotionally appealed to the masses to overthrow the "old gang," the political rings, and the trusts, and he was elected.

As governor, Long forced New Orleans Public Service, Inc., to provide the Crescent City with inexpensive natural gas. As pledged, he provided all school children with free textbooks, financed by an increase in the severance tax. He made textbooks available to private and parochial schools, as well as public, arguing that he was furnishing the books directly to the children and therefore not violating the constitutional prohibition of public aid to religious institutions. Under Long's supervision the legislature passed a constitutional amendment permitting the issue of $30-million-worth of bonds; the money was to be used to build free roads and bridges. The legislature repealed the tobacco tax, and it increased appropriations for the state's eleemosynary institutions. In 1928 Louisiana had 296 miles of concrete roads, 35 miles of asphalt roads, and 5,728 miles of gravel roads within the state highway system. By the time of Long's assassination in 1935, these figures had been increased to 2,446, 1,308, and 9,629, respectively. In 1928 there were three bridges within the state highway system; there were over forty major bridges in the state by 1935. Long's free textbook program stimulated a 20 percent jump in public school enrollment, and he greatly increased appropriations for higher education. As a result of his efforts, one hundred thousand adult illiterates of both races enrolled in free night schools. State hospitals and other institutions received substantially larger appropriations. All of this was based on sound financial practices including taxes and bonds. While business progressives professed a belief in the regulation of public utilities, in good roads, in more support for charitable institutions, and in educational development, none could have guessed the extent to which a Huey Long could bring about such changes. But although he had developed a powerful political machine, there were significant anti-Long forces in the state. Long's most significant contributions to Louisiana politics were the revitalization of state politics and the development of a lasting bifactionalism that has affected the state to the present day.

Bifactionalism was not as distinct in the remainder of the South as it was in Louisiana. In most southern states the business progressives constituted only one of several groups contending for political office and power. This multifactionalism tended to keep any single group from dominating state politics. In most states the business progressives were forced to share political power with the other groups; but they were a significant factor in southern politics of the twenties. During that decade the South's industrial development was little short of phenomenal. Progress in education, transportation, public services, and governmental efficiency was in large measure a result of their efforts.

RELIGION AND RACE

Business progressivism and political conservatism existed side by side in the South in the 1920s. While the business progressives were engaging in mild reforms, southern conservatives fulminated against change. Conservative politicians probably reflected the sentiments of the majority of the southern populace more accurately than the progressives. This was especially true in the famous evolution controversies in the twenties, which emphasized how closely religious fundamentalism and political conservatism were woven together in the region.

Orthodox Protestantism had been strong in the United States throughout the nineteenth century. When the Progressive movement was at its height, when the nation was experiencing the growing pains of a gigantic industrial and technological age, and when religious liberalism seemed to be making progress, many Americans drew back in revulsion. They feared change and the possibility of change, and they voiced a need for a return to absolutes. At a national convention in 1910, conservative religious leaders in the United States outlined the doctrines that they believed to be basic to the Christian faith, introducing the word *fundamental* into American religious nomenclature.

Although the fundamentalist movement was national in scope, the South was the region of its greatest vitality. Although southerners had long cherished its basic tenets, the movement gained strength during the unsettling war years, and during the 1920s thousands of southerners grasped at religious fundamentalism as their only hope of stability in a constantly changing world. Unalterably committed to biblical absolutes, southern Protestant Christians had long opposed Charles Darwin's evolutionary theories about animals and men, which appeared to contradict the first chapter of Genesis, detailing the act of Creation. In the early 1920s several denominations in the South officially pronounced that according to Genesis man was the special creation of God, and they rejected every theory that "man originated in, or came by way of, a lower animal ancestry." No large religious denomination officially requested state assemblies to legislate against the teaching of evolution in the public schools of the southern states, but the fundamentalist milieu was so pervasive in the 1920s that demands for antievolution laws were inevitable.

In 1922 in the border state of Kentucky, antievolutionists made their first major effort to enact a law supporting their views, but the bill was voted down by slender margins in both houses of the state legislature. In that same year, fundamentalists made a similar attempt to outlaw the teaching of Darwinism in South Carolina's and Georgia's public schools, but they failed. In 1923 similar bills failed to receive approval in the Tennessee and Alabama legislatures, and the Texas house passed but its senate failed to vote on a bill forbidding the teaching of the Darwinian hypothesis "as a fact" in state-supported schools. Almost identical with the Texas resolution was one approved by the Florida state legislature in 1923, expressing the "sense" that public school teachers should not teach atheism, agnosticism, or Darwinism "as true," but the resolution provided for no penalties for offending teachers, and professors at the University of Florida openly ignored the "sense" of the legislature. As the antievolution campaign became nationwide, controversies arose in the legislatures of northern and western states, such as Maine, Minnesota, Oregon, and California, and the border states of West Virginia, Missouri, and Oklahoma. A major success for the antievolutionists came in 1923 when the Oklahoma legislature passed a free school book law stipulating that no textbook should be adopted if it taught the Darwinian theory of creation. When North Carolina's and Texas's state legislatures refused to enact statutes, the state boards of education ordered the elimination of textbooks espousing Darwinism.

The antievolutionists increased their pressures during 1925, but their efforts were unsuccessful in both the North Carolina and Georgia legislatures, and they failed to supplement Florida's

A *New York Times Magazine* feature on the Scopes evolution trial, 5 July 1925. (© by The New York Times Company. Reprinted by permission.)

earlier resolution. But in the same year Tennessee passed an ironclad statute forbidding the teaching of Darwinian theory in public schools and requiring fines for teachers who broke the law. John T. Scopes lost his sensational test case in 1926. Antievolutionists introduced bills similar to Tennessee's in the legislatures of Kentucky and Louisiana. Neither passed; but the following year the Mississippi legislature easily enacted one, heartily approved by the governor, allowing fines of up to $500 for violators.

Maximum efforts to secure legislative restrictions against teaching evolutionary theory came in 1927, when bills condemning it were introduced in fourteen states, including North Carolina, South Carolina, Florida, Alabama, and Arkansas, as well as the border states of Oklahoma, Missouri, and West Virginia. None passed, but the margin of defeat was rather narrow in several instances. After the Arkansas legislature defeated a bill, the electorate approved a law in a general referendum in 1928. But its success came in the midst of a general decline in antievolutionist agitation, and it was the last major triumph of those who sought statutory approval of religious beliefs.

Between 1922 and 1928, four southern states enacted antievolution laws. The remaining southern states at least considered similar bills, in some cases only narrowly defeating them, indicating the strength of fundamentalist sentiment in the South. In fact, it is likely that more laws would have been passed had other states besides Arkansas permitted the electorate to decide the issue. Members of the state legislatures were often of educated, middle-class backgrounds who voted their own predispositions rather than yielding to the pressures of their less educated, lower-class constituents; the latter group contained the hard-core fundamentalists. But in any case, the antievolution crusade revealed the powerful impact of religious conservatism on the South's political processes.

The growing strength and brief domination of the Ku Klux Klan in parts of the South during the twenties was another indication of the presence of a strong conservative and reactionary element in southern politics. The Klan of the Reconstruction Era had developed from white southern frustration with the outcome of the Civil War and opposition to the emerging role of the black man in southern society. Trumpeting white supremacy, the Klan lasted officially for only a few years, after which it went underground for several more years before it finally died. A second Klan was founded in 1915 by Colonel William J.

Simmons, when he and fifteen other Georgians met at the top of
Stone Mountain near Atlanta to dedicate themselves to the
maintenance of white supremacy. The revived KKK linked the
doctrine of Anglo-Saxon superiority to nativism, patriotism,
Protestantism, and morality and thus had mass appeal in the
1920s. Through publicity and organization, the Klan acquired a
large following and national influence. The Klan inevitably
became involved in politics as a manifestation of a conservative
society, and for a few years it developed strong political organizations in several southern states as well as in northern states such as
Indiana and Oregon and border-state Oklahoma.

The Klan was strongest politically in Texas and Arkansas.
Having gained control of Democratic party machinery in Texas,
its members swept the lower house of the legislature and elected a
host of local candidates in 1922. In that year Texas had the
dubious honor of sending to Washington Earle B. Mayfield, the
first genuine Klan senator. The secret organization shortly
reached its peak in Texas and by the fall of 1923 it had lost much
of its political clout. When anti-Klan candidates won major state
offices in the election of 1924, the Klan became politically
toothless and the Lone Star State became one of the most
anti-Klan states in the Union. After the brief Klan interlude
Texans returned to their preferred traditional leaders and politics
as usual.

The KKK won nearly every office in Arkansas in 1922,
electing members and sympathizers not only to local positions but
also to the House of Representatives in Washington. Yet despite
the large number of Klan officeholders, opposition to the Klan
grew within the state's Democratic party. In the 1924 election the
retiring governor gave his support to Tom J. Terral, reportedly a
former Klansman whom the Invisible Empire bitterly opposed.
Terral was elected but so were several Klan-supported statewide
candidates. When the Arkansas Klan split under the pressures of
internal friction, however, its political strength was reduced and
by the end of 1925 the Klan in the Razorback State was impotent.
Politicians were soon running for office on the claim that they had
not been or were no longer members of the secret organization.

The Klan was moderately successful in politics in Louisiana,
Mississippi, Tennessee, and Alabama. It had local influence in
Louisiana, particularly in the northwestern parishes near Arkansas, but it never acquired the statewide power that it had wielded
in Texas and Arkansas. When violence flared in the northern

parishes, Governor John Parker used the state militia to forestall warfare between the Klan and its opponents. He also secured passage of a law requiring the KKK to register its membership rolls with the state. The organization was not daunted, but the murder of two anti-Klansmen, even though the murderers were never identified and brought to justice, brought the Louisiana Klan into ill repute and it did not fare well in the 1924 elections; its influence soon waned.

In Mississippi the Klan was mainly an anti-Catholic organization, and in a state with a small Catholic population, it appealed to Masons but few others. Respected former Senators Williams and LeRoy Percy took the lead in publicly opposing the Klan, and it never became a potent force in the Magnolia State. In 1923 the Mississippi organization supported James K. Vardaman in an unsuccessful bid for a Senate seat, and it failed again in its attempt to unseat longtime Vicksburg congressman, John W. Collier. The highpoint in the Mississippi Klan's life came in 1924 when it dominated the state's delegation to the Democratic presidential nominating convention, but even that delegation included several outspoken non-Klansmen, including Senator Pat Harrison. After the failure of the Klan's exhaustive drive to elect a sheriff in Greenville, its remaining strength was entirely dissipated.

Most of the Tennessee KKK's power was concentrated in the western and eastern edges of the state. The Invisible Empire made its most strenuous political efforts in the Chattanooga and Memphis municipal elections in 1923, but it was defeated in both cities. The Klan remained an important political factor in the state, though not the decisive one. In 1924 the group helped defeat Senator John Shields, and it worked for the reelection of Governor Peay who had won its approval by refusing to support anti-Klan moves; but the Klan passed its peak in Tennessee in 1924.

The powerful opposition of Senator Underwood held Alabama's Klan in check. His prestige and influence at the national level was great, and the Klan hesitated to oppose him openly. When Underwood failed in his bid for the Democratic presidential nomination in 1924, however, the Klan had reason for hope and openly attacked the elderly senator, probably influencing Underwood's decision not to try for reelection in 1926. The Klan was jubilant when it helped elect a young sympathizer to replace Underwood; he was Hugo Black, whose Klan affiliation later embarrassed him when he was appointed to the United States

Supreme Court. In 1926 the Klan's support was crucial in the victories of Klansmen Bibb Graves and Charles C. McCall for governor and attorney general of Alabama, respectively. The Klan was then at its height in that state, but it was soon overstepping its bounds; the press became more courageous in its exposés, the new attorney general openly broke with his former allies, and by the end of 1927 the Alabama Klan had begun to crumble.

The Klan manifested much less strength in the Atlantic seaboard states of Virginia, North Carolina, South Carolina, and Florida. Its presence did not seriously challenge the Flood-Byrd Democratic machine that dominated Virginia politics in the twenties. Most of the newspapers of the state either criticized or ignored the Invisible Empire, whose candidates were unsuccessful almost everywhere. While the organization had support in some of the new industrial cities of the Old Dominion, its political power was never great in the state as a whole. The conservative machine had many backers who were attracted to the reactionary Klan, but the fact that no transfer of allegiance occurred is a tribute to Virginia Democratic loyalty to the dominant political organization. Whatever its ideology, the Klan represented the political "outs" in Virginia, and the "ins" were strong enough to maintain their positions and power. The Klan elected no member or supporter to high office either in North or South Carolina, and likewise it made little headway at the state level in Florida, even though Sidney J. Catts had become governor in 1917 after running on a platform with an anti-Catholic plank. The Florida KKK hoped for a statewide political appeal that never developed.

In Georgia, the headquarters of the national Klan, the organization won numerous smaller offices in 1920, especially in Fulton County (Atlanta). In 1922 it staunchly opposed anti-Klan Governor Thomas W. Hardwick and successfully supported former state attorney general Clifford Walker for governor. The organization also counted among its friends the state superintendents of education and agriculture and the elder Richard B. Russell, the respected chief justice of Georgia's supreme court. In the state's 1924 presidential primary election, the Klan supported McAdoo against Underwood and was probably responsible for McAdoo's victory. Opposition had been rising against the Klan in Georgia, however, and soon the group was decidedly on the wane. The harsh light of publicity, vigorous opposition from leading newspapers, and anti-Klan stands by Georgia politicians such as Hardwick were instrumental in its demise. Pro-Klan Governor

Walker, whom the press dubbed "Kautious Kleagle Kliff," was powerless by the end of his second term in office. In 1926 the Klan opposed Senator Walter George because of his support of the World Court, and it campaigned vigorously for an entire slate of Klan sympathizers for state and national offices. Not a single Klan candidate won. George was overwhelmingly reelected to the Senate, and the Klan's candidate for governor ran last in the Democratic primary. Klan-inspired violence continued in Georgia, but the Klan was politically dead.

Although Klan political strength rose and fell in the various southern states at different times and to different levels, the organization was a potent force in the twenties in every southern state, particularly in local politics. Policemen, municipal committees, mayors, and dogcatchers were often Klansmen or dependent upon Klansmen's favor. To say that the group was "the electorate" at the precinct level, as some have believed, is an exaggeration, but without question it appealed to the needs and prejudices of many southerners in a postwar era of change.

The Ku Klux Klan of the 1920s was less interested in the black man than was the Klan of Reconstruction days. But its vehement anti-Catholicism, patriotism, and defense of morality did not mean the secret organization totally ignored the region's largest minority group. Like the earlier KKK, the Klan of the twenties engaged in violence, much of which was directed toward blacks. Its emphasis upon Anglo-Saxon superiority, its willingness to use physical force to intimidate the black populace, and its interest in keeping blacks politically ineffective combined to do great harm to the black man. But other southerners, including anti-Klansmen and non-Klansmen, were also antiblack and the black voter in the South in the twenties had many obstacles with which to contend.

In the first decade and a half of the twentieth century, political parties in southern states had set up primary elections that excluded most blacks from voting. Even though many blacks had gained some economic advantage during the First World War, the political realm remained closed to them. After the war, white southerners moved to sanction the informal white primary with an assertion of its legality and to make it even more effective. Mistakenly believing that party primaries were beyond the reach of the Supreme Court, the Texas legislature in 1923 enacted a law providing that "in no event shall a negro be eligible to participate in a Democratic primary election held in the State of Texas, and should a negro vote in a Democratic primary election, such ballot shall be void and election officials shall not count the same." Texas blacks could not allow such a brazen attempt to disfranchise them to go uncontested, and soon L. A. Nixon, a black physician in El Paso, tried to vote in a Democratic primary election. When he was denied a ballot, Dr. Nixon sued an election judge named Herndon for damages on the grounds that the state statute violated the Fourteenth and Fifteenth Amendments of the Constitution. The case reached the Supreme Court, which ruled that the act was void because it denied the equal protection of the laws guaranteed in the Fourteenth Amendment. The Court stated that it was "hard to imagine a more direct and obvious infringement" of the Fourteenth Amendment, which had been adopted "with special intent to protect the blacks from discrimination against them." This was a victory for Nixon, but since the Court did not consider the validity of the Texas law in regard to the Fifteenth Amendment, which prohibits denial of the right to vote based on race or color, it avoided the question of whether party primaries could be controlled by the national government.

Nixon v. *Herndon* (1927) was a hollow victory for black voters generally. Within a few months of the decision the Texas legislature repealed its law barring blacks in Democratic primaries and enacted a resolution that authorized "every political party in this State through its State Executive Committee . . . to prescribe the qualifications of its own members." As soon as this law became effective, the state executive committee of the Democratic party adopted a resolution that "all white Democrats who are qualified under the constitution and laws of Texas . . . and none other, [shall] be allowed to participate in the primary elections." Denied the right to vote once again, Dr. Nixon brought a second suit for damages.

The defendant in *Nixon* v. *Condon* (1932) argued that the plaintiff had no complaint: Nixon had been excluded by the action of a private party and this did not constitute a violation of the Fourteenth Amendment, since that amendment was designed to ensure against state abuse of the equal protection clause. Although the Supreme Court again refused to rule on whether a private political party could deny membership to blacks, it noted that the Texas Democratic party's state executive committee did not have the power to exclude blacks from the party: "Whatever power of exclusion has been exercised by the members of the committee has come to them . . . not as delegates of the party, but as the delegates of the state." The Court ruled that the committee had acted because of power granted to it by the state legislature; therefore, the state of Texas, through the executive committee of the Democratic party, was guilty of discrimination —not the private Democratic party itself. In short, when the executive committee prohibited Nixon's participation in the primary election, the state violated the equal protection clause of the Constitution. This decision affected not only Texas, but also every other southern state. In 1930 the Democratic party had denied blacks the voting privilege by statewide rule in eight former Confederate states and by county and city rules in the remaining three—Florida, North Carolina, and Tennessee.

During most of this period of legal skirmishing, the majority of the black voters in the South were registered Republicans; their loyalty to the party of emancipation in a region where one-party politics prevailed did not enhance their political position. As a registered Republican the black man was unable to vote in the Democratic primaries, and in general elections Republican votes were ineffectual for lack of numerical strength. In addition, southern white Republicans were as race conscious as their Democratic opponents, and they made no efforts to embrace their black political allies. Indeed, on occasion they made statements as racist as any the Democrats were famous for making. In 1920 a Republican candidate for governor of North Carolina publicly stated his opposition to blacks voting. A few years later, that state's Republican party chairman proudly proclaimed that blacks "have taken no part in the affairs of the Republican party since I have been Chairman." In 1921 a Republican ran for governor of Virginia with the promise to exclude blacks from office. In other elections in southern states in the 1920s the Republican candidates were so "lily-white" that on the few occasions when black Republicans ran for office they had to do so as Independents.

Nor did the national Republican party in the 1920s give southern blacks cause for hope. In 1921 President Harding lectured the South on the subject of race relations. He stated that the key to racial harmony was for both races to "stand uncompromisingly against every suggestion of social equality," to recognize "a fundamental, eternal and inescapable difference." Acknowledging that the black man should vote "when he is fit to vote" and should have equal opportunity "in precisely the same way and to the same extent . . . as between members of the same race," the president qualified his statement so that "equal opportunity" did not mean that both races "would become equally educated within a generation or two generations or ten generations." Harding concluded that a black "should seek to be the best possible black man, and not the best possible imitation of a white man." Such statements only served to strengthen feelings that blacks were unwelcome in either party.

Republicans in southern states had little hope of winning elections in the 1920s; they remained organized primarily to obtain federal patronage, which invariably went to loyal white party members. In the past coalitions of white and "black-and-tan" Republicans had shared federal offices in the South, but in a decade noted for reactionary racism, the legitimacy of these arrangements was questioned. In a final coup de grâce, the Republican presidential candidate, Herbert Hoover, ignored the black-and-tan factions in the 1928 presidential campaign and then later denied blacks patronage in an attempt "to build up a Republican party in the South such as would commend itself to the [white] citizens of those states." Blacks complained but to no avail.

Local elections sometimes provided blacks with opportunities for political influence, especially in Virginia and Texas. Occasionally municipal reform issues, disputed bond referendums, and school elections brought out enough black votes for the margin of victory or defeat. In 1921 black voters in Atlanta supported and thus helped pass a $4 million school bond issue, but only after they had received a pledge that one-fourth of the total would be spent on black schools. In Nashville in 1921 and Savannah in 1923, whites openly solicited black votes on behalf of municipal reform measures. These examples of black involvement were rare, however, and they only emphasize that blacks had little or no political power. The southern politicians of the twenties were no less committed to minimal black political involvement than were their prewar predecessors. The subject did not dominate their politics—because they believed the prewar Progressives had "solved" the problem—but they were conscious of it, and the state statutes, the court cases, and the presence of the Ku Klux Klan were reminders of the black thread running through southern politics after the Civil War.

For the South, as for the nation, the initial years of the twentieth century had seen the Progressive crusade, and if southerners looked upon Progressive ideas somewhat differently than did other Americans, the basic interest and concern—and at times the almost evangelical fervor—were there. Just before the war, however, progressivism was beginning to burn itself out; the reforms, especially during the first year or so of the Wilson administration in Washington, had been notable enough that a time of rest was almost visibly at hand. Then the embroilments of neutrality during the world war that had begun in 1914 began to impinge upon the consciousness of all Americans, southerners not least, and soon the country was at war.

The importance of the war for the South was far more than military; it produced economic and social and even humanitarian changes. The war offered opportunities to whites and blacks alike that changed the entire range of anticipations in the region. People went North to the factories, and some southerners returned; others, many of them blacks, did not. Northerners came south to help populate the army camps. The influence of the war continued into the postwar decade. During the twenties, the spirit of change was becoming evident everywhere.

Even more change seemed imminent in 1929; but the stock market collapse, as all Americans would learn, would be no temporary setback to progress. It presaged a worldwide economic downturn that lasted throughout the thirties, ending only with another world war. The Great Depression was one of the greatest domestic disasters in American history; its effects on the South were shattering.

THREE

The
Great
Depression

The United States in the 1920s achieved the highest standard of living any nation had ever known. National income jumped; wages were high; the work week had been shortened; demand for American consumer goods was great. The American industrial complex was operating more efficiently as mass production techniques were refined; industrial production almost doubled during the decade. The building and construction industry boomed, as large and small cities rebuilt their interiors and erected skyscrapers. Automobiles, highway construction, and electrical demands added to the production circus. The prosperity of the 1920s produced the contagious feeling that everyone could—and would—be rich.

The American economy was functioning on borrowed time in the 1920s, however. Its superstructure was built upon weak and continually sagging foundations. The nation's total income was badly distributed; technological unemployment resulted from the multiplication of labor-saving machines; a minority interested in siphoning off profits for themselves dominated the corporations; inadequate regulation and bad management plagued the banking system; the national government ignored its responsibility to regulate business; the business world refused to accept any effective measures for the relief of agriculture that continually overproduced; international trade was out of balance; and the overoptimistic public speculated indiscriminately in stocks and bonds.

The South in the twentieth century had already discovered that it could not live apart from the nation as a whole. As if the lessons of the Progressive movement and the war were not enough, however, the South was once again—this time more violently than ever—forced to recognize its involvement in the affairs of the rest of the country. When the stock market crash and the Great Depression spread out from Wall Street in New York, the South felt the jolt.

The business depression that began in 1929 affected the entire economy of the nation, but because the South was so largely agricultural its economy suffered far more. Agriculture, not least southern agriculture, was perhaps the last refuge of the nation's individualists. Here had been the section of the economy where individual producers acted largely by and for themselves, refusing to worry about the movements of markets, national or world. When the Great Depression struck economies everywhere, not merely in the United States, the South's agricultural markets began to disappear. Southern farmers found themselves in straits of a sort that were beyond memory and even beyond history. By the year 1932, which was the depression's worst year, the South was in an almost unimaginable crisis of poverty, accompanied by something approaching social and political despair.

THE BEGINNINGS OF TROUBLE

Agriculture in the United States, and not least in the South, had been in the doldrums ever since the end of the world war, and in that sense at least the coming of the depression to the states of the South was a continuation of the troubles of preceding years. A price break in the cotton market had resulted in demands to cut production in 1921, and a Cotton Acreage Reduction Convention had met in Memphis to encourage reduced planting in the spring of that year. The Memphis convention, the boll weevil, and bad weather combined to limit the cotton crop, but decreased production did not solve the farmers' basic problems. Cotton growers' associations were then established in several states; convinced that unscientific farming, the crop lien system, and a less than satisfactory marketing system were responsible for agricultural woes, they favored rural credit, holding operations, and crop limitation and diversification. The associations emphasized the need for good business operations, including cooperative marketing, direct selling, better warehouse facilities, pest control, improved seeds, and more foreign markets. They stimulated a cooperative marketing movement of considerable proportions in the early 1920s, reminiscent of the cotton mill campaigns of the South in the late nineteenth century. The associations hoped to secure a monopoly on the marketing of cotton, but they marketed no more than 10 percent of the crop in any state.

The impact of economic forces upon the southern farmer and his family during the 1920s was notable. The severity of the economic failures of staple agriculture in the South translated into effects on human beings was frightening. In each successive year of the 1920s the blight of sharecropping and farm tenancy affected greater numbers of human beings; never before were there so many landless farmers or so great a mire of rural poverty.

While conditions were bad for the southern farmer throughout the 1920s, they worsened after the stock market crash. Because of increasing demand, cotton prices had risen as high as 20.19 cents in 1927, but they had settled back to less than 17 cents in 1929. Then came real disaster: they fell to 9.46 cents in 1930 and 5.66 cents in 1931. In June 1932 the price fell to 4.6 cents on the New Orleans Cotton Exchange, the lowest level since 1894. Tobacco fared no better; for three years in a row, tobacco prices dropped an average of almost 4 cents a pound after having sold for 18.3 cents a pound in 1929. In 1930 Louisiana sugar sold for less than 3 cents a pound, 2 cents of which amounted to government support.

Before 1929, worsening agricultural conditions had not unduly affected regional industry and business, but after the crash all sectors of the southern economy felt the impact of agriculture's debilitating sickness. Most directly affected was textile manufacturing. Despite the lack of markets, textile mills continued to pour out yards of unwanted cloth. Even though cotton prices and labor costs were low, the textile manufacturers found their own profit margins dwindling, and soon their gross returns were hardly enough to cover their costs. The depression hit the rural mills and small towns first, but as it deepened, the South's urban areas and commercial centers also suffered. Each year trading and sales declined in almost every commodity, and in most categories commerce in the southern states deteriorated more than in the nation as a whole.

The general economic slump affected transportation and banking. Railroads began to earn less than the minimum permitted by the Interstate Commerce Commission, and by July 1933 seven of the twenty-one Class I railroads, which controlled more than a quarter of the region's tracks were in receivership. In 1929 the South's proportion of the nation's banking resources had been 9.7 percent; in 1935 it was down to 8.7, a total decline of nearly $2 billion. Southern banks suffered greatly because so many of them were undercapitalized, poorly managed, and inadequately regulated. An Atlanta banker noted that many failed "because the community in which they operated failed." Banks were left with worthless mortgages on land, crops, and businesses; bankruptcy filings usually followed foreclosure proceedings. Other areas of the South had shared the boom of the 1920s: Florida had fast become an attractive retirement and real estate investment region, while the mountain areas of Virginia and North and South Carolina had attracted tourists and other resort seekers. With the advent of the depression, however, real estate values slipped, tourism dwindled to a trickle, and developers and promoters were left with nothing to show for all their advertising and promotion efforts. In 1934 one well-informed observer estimated that 90 percent of the money invested in southern real estate speculation was unrecoverable.

Related to these economic conditions was the inevitable drop in per capita income. The South's per capita income had traditionally been lower than the nation's in the first place—in 1929 it was slightly less than half the national average—and when the depression came it sank at a faster rate than the national decline. By 1932 the South's per capita income was about half its 1929 figure. In addition, many southerners were totally unemployed and others only partially employed as a result of the crisis. Employment in the South as a whole in 1933 was only about 60 percent of the 1929 level. President Hoover had campaigned in 1928 on a prosperity ticket calling for two chickens in every pot, but by 1930 many families would have been happy to have eggs on the table. In 1931 a Red Cross worker visited forty families in rural Arkansas and found 60 percent of them with virtually no food in their homes; five families had no food at all. President Roosevelt was later to assure the nation that no one would starve, but he was not familiar with the most poverty-stricken regions of the South.

Local and county governments in the South attempted to remedy the dire economic conditions, although their efforts amounted to something like placing a gauze bandage on a ruptured artery. They directed much of their attention to the problem of unemployment, but they were unable to cope with massive human distress. Town, city, and county treasuries were quickly drained when governmental units employed the fathers of hungry children on road-repairing projects, parks and recreation crews, and minor construction projects. No matter how concerned and conscientious local officials were, they simply did not have the resources to meet the needs of the destitute. In January 1931, Birmingham, Alabama, voted a bond issue of $500,000 to pay for additional men to work in the city's public parks. Even though the workers received only 25 cents an hour, nearly half of the money had been devoured by September. In the same year the city of Little Rock, Arkansas, appropriated $20,000, supplemented by $25,000 in private contributions, for emergency relief work; but within three months the money was gone and the men who had been hired for made-work projects had to be released. Louisville, Atlanta, New Orleans, and other southern cities had the same experience. Jacksonville, Florida, fared better because of the philanthropy of Alfred I. DuPont, who dispatched trucks each morning to transport unemployed men to work in the city's parks for $1.25 per day; some days his payroll ran as high as $400. DuPont continued his assistance until New Deal agencies took over in 1933; but his personal efforts were exceptions to the rule.

Some leaders in the urban centers tried to stimulate a back-to-the-farm movement to rid their jurisdictions of unemployed persons. Rooted in a rural culture, these urban politicians somehow believed that the farm areas could serve as safety valves for the worsening conditions in the cities. The *Atlanta Journal* agreed and wrote, "Georgia's 50,000 abandoned farms offer a haven for those who are dispiritedly walking the streets." The Atlanta Chamber of Commerce sponsored a program to send nearly sixty families back to the farm. Muscogee County, Georgia, Houston, Texas, and Greenville, South Carolina, initiated similar projects; but all were counterproductive. Many people in urban areas had come there in the first place because economic distress had driven them off the farms. However ideal the farm might be as a place to live, the reality of the depression dictated that it was no refuge for the surplus unemployed.

Governors and other state leaders often expressed the belief that the unemployed were themselves responsible for their destitute conditions, and that they simply needed to try harder to find work. Texas Governor Ross Sterling suggested that people who did not use "what means they may have" were responsible for their own improvidence. State politicians were inclined to agree with a small businessman who wrote Texas Congressman Sam Rayburn that "most of the unemployed men on the road are hoboes just because they want to be and this unemployed publicity has made it easy for them." Individualism was certainly a part of southern and American traditions; but that statement hardly took into consideration the presence of powerful collective social and economic forces. The American work ethic seemed somehow inapplicable at a time when a fifth of the population struggled desperately against real starvation and a larger fraction had only a minimum of the necessities of life. When it became clear that local relief funds and efforts were not solving the problems, state leaders were compelled to give attention to the needy, despite their philosophical leanings; but states were not much better equipped for the job than the local governmental units. State treasuries were not bountiful in the first place, and relief aid to the destitute cut deeply into the coffers.

When state leaders realized the magnitude of the problem, they sought ways to solve the money crisis. One way was to be more efficient regarding state expenditures. The depression had stopped the expansive impulse of business progressivism, but it did not stifle the progressive interest in governmental efficiency. State leaders effected reform measures to tighten state finances. Virginia's Governor John G. Pollard and his legislature cut appropriations by more than $7 million. Governor O. Max Gardner saved a similar amount in North Carolina, mainly by governmental centralization efforts including the consolidation of the state's three major public universities. Elected governor of Georgia in 1930 on a platform of economy and efficiency, Richard B. Russell, Jr., saved nearly $1 million by reorganizing ninety state agencies into nineteen departments. The Texas legislature in 1933 reduced appropriations by about 20 percent, and other states

Farm Security Administration photographs of life in the South during the Great Depression. (Library of Congress)

followed the general pattern. A second way to solve the states' financial problems was to collect more taxes. Various southern states turned to the general sales tax when other measures were not effective enough. Despite its regressive characteristics and the strong opposition of retail businessmen, the practicality of the sales tax was undisputed. It brought millions of dollars into state treasuries when they were desperately needed to finance projects that in the past had been recognized as the province of lesser jurisdictions. Historically, local units had received most of the combined total of state and local revenues, but with the advent of the depression and the widespread use of the sales tax, the tax structure was reversed and states began to take the lion's share. Yet even then the states were unable to solve the economic problems, although they had accepted responsibility for the job.

State attempts to overcome the cotton crisis illustrate the impotence of state government when a major problem arose. State leaders correctly believed that if cotton could be sold at a reasonable price, many problems such as unemployment and virtual starvation could be solved before they appeared. The way to raise the price of cotton was to produce less. Huey Long and his pliant legislature foolishly passed an unenforceable law prohibiting the "planting, gathering, and ginning of cotton in 1932." Other states took less drastic action. In Texas Governor Sterling sponsored a measure to limit cotton acreage in 1932 and 1933 to 30 percent of the previous year's crop. The governor of Arkansas favored a crop reduction scheme, and the Mississippi and South Carolina legislatures passed laws similar to Texas's. When the Texas Supreme Court declared that state's plan unconstitutional, however, the reduction movement ended.

Despite the efforts of city and state governments to fight the depression, conditions worsened. They were not financially equipped to handle an economic crisis of this magnitude.

A NEW DEAL

Although southerners and their state leaders had long believed in states' rights, preferring not to have the national government involved in their political and economic domains, common sense and economic necessity dictated the violation of old traditions. The farmers' economic problems invited political solutions, and national senators and representatives from rural states formed a Farm Bloc during the agricultural crisis of 1920–21. Between 1921 and 1923 the Farm Bloc successfully backed or led the fight for measures such as the Emergency Tariff of 1921, which protected farm products; the Grain Futures Trading Act; the Capper-Volstead Cooperative Marketing Act, which exempted agricultural cooperatives from the antitrust laws; and the Intermediate Credit Act of 1923, which extended credit under the Federal Reserve System and established intermediate credit banks for medium-term loans. Throughout the 1920s farm representatives in Washington suggested that farm surpluses be dumped abroad, but the various McNary-Haugen bills designed for that purpose either failed in Congress or were vetoed by the president.

Many southerners favored the rather limited attempts of President Hoover to solve the farm problem. Just before the stock market crash his administration had passed the Agricultural Marketing Act of 1929 which embodied Hoover's concept of "orderly" cooperative marketing of agricultural products. It created the Federal Farm Reserve Board funded with $500 million to assist cooperatives and "stablization corporations" in buying surpluses and thus keeping the market price for farm products at a reasonably high level. The Farm Board's efforts, limited mainly to cotton and wheat, got under way just as the Great Depression began in October 1929, but prices did not respond to the board's activities. While the states' reduction actions were proving unsuccessful, the Farm Board began slowing down its purchases of surpluses, and cotton prices sank lower and lower. Despite its ineffectiveness, the Farm Board by its presence suggested to southerners that the solution to economic problems might lie in forgetting traditional resistance to federal help and paved the way for later acceptance of the New Deal.

When President Franklin D. Roosevelt took office in March 1933, farm relief was prominent in his plan to improve the nation's economic conditions. Extreme poverty and economic depression in the rural South forced the new administration to focus its attention on the region. Many of the New Deal measures were directed toward the agricultural South and the president was to label it the "nation's no. 1 economic problem." Tenancy, inadequate marketing procedures, lack of capital and credit, low income, and the pitfalls of the single-crop system constituted the basic problems southern agriculture had faced since the Civil War. New Deal legislation attempted to solve those problems by extending credit, adjusting debts, artificially raising farm prices, instituting soil conservation programs, and placing acreage controls on major crops. Southerners on Capitol Hill eagerly drafted or supported bills dealing with these matters. The Senate and House majority leaders, Joseph T. Robinson of Arkansas and Joseph Byrns of Tennessee, gave the president full support and were effective tacticians in the legislative chambers. In crucial positions, southern committee chairmen used their power and parliamentary skills to guide specific bills under their jurisdiction through the Senate or the House.

One of the most important New Deal agricultural measures for the South and the nation was the Agricultural Adjustment Act of 1933, whose primary objective was to raise farm prices. Government contracts were to provide benefit payments to farmers who voluntarily restricted crops and acreage. The act was not passed until May of 1933, after many thousands of acres of cotton and tobacco had been planted and after the spring's pigs and calves had been born. Artificial scarcity and the resultant higher prices could be achieved only by slaughtering the excess animals and plowing under the rows of surplus cotton and tobacco. Farmers who cooperated with the government's program for crop reduction found benefit payment checks—eventually totaling millions of dollars overall—in their seldom-used mailboxes.

To what extent the agricultural programs of the New Deal helped the South remains a disputed question. Not a few farmers survived the depression years only because of government subsistence; but at the end of the 1930s the South's chief occupation was still in distress. Hardest hit was the man at the bottom of the economic structure: the tenant. If some landlords received benefit payments for crop reduction, the tenant often did not. Always a marginal farmer, he profited little from the government's various plans and proposals to assist agriculture. The efforts of the Resettlement Administration to withdraw from cultivation many acres of marginal land in the South and to relocate tenants elsewhere were not highly successful. Because fewer acres were being planted, fewer laborers were required to cultivate and harvest them. Thousands of tenants, the majority of them blacks, were made jobless, adding to the already lengthy relief roles of counties and towns. One of the great millstones around the neck of the South, tenancy reached its peak between 1930 and 1935. Statistics heralding its decline after 1935 were no cause for rejoicing by those who had long deplored the presence of the system in the region; the circumstances that inaugurated the decline were as unwelcome as the continued existence of tenancy itself. Agricultural conditions failed to improve significantly, but southern farmers recognized that without the New Deal they were potentially in even worse trouble, and they generally supported Roosevelt.

Southern small town and city dwellers and their elected representatives were nearly as supportive of Roosevelt and the New Deal as their rural cousins. Members of southern labor unions benefited from New Deal legislation that set minimum wages and maximum hours, guaranteed collective bargaining, and established a federal mediation board. Small businessmen often complained about the National Recovery Administration: its price policies, its edicts, its domination by large businesses, and its administrative bureaucracy. But the NRA gave jobs to some two million workers, it slowed the nation's deflationary spiral, it tamed business competition, and it improved business ethics. Southern businessmen recognized these achievements and continued to vote for Roosevelt.

A few southern governors attempted to implement "little New Deals" in their states. Governors Olin D. Johnston of South Carolina, James V. Allred of Texas, and Eurith D. ("Ed") Rivers of Georgia encouraged the passage of workmen's compensation laws, forty-hour weeks for laborers, free textbooks for public school children, increased financing and reorganization of state public health and mental health agencies, increased cooperation between the state and federal highway and relief officials, and new systems of welfare distribution. Some governors also favored and implemented the establishment of the social security system in their states. Much of this legislation at the state level was in the tradition of the progressivism of the previous decade as well as being imitative of the national New Deal program.

An exception to the pro–New Dealers was Governor Eugene Talmadge of Georgia, an outspoken critic of Roosevelt and his programs. He protested loudly the administration's relief, wage, and highway policies. He was particularly incensed with federal relief officials, and he often harassed those in his state. When he was asked how the unemployed should be handled, he shouted, "Let 'em starve." Part of the reason for his unhappiness with the New Deal related to race; he objected to federal social workers' attempts to provide blacks with adequate relief payments. Talmadge cut state expenditures, dried up public services, reduced legislative appropriations, vetoed old-age pensions and free textbooks; but all the while he continued to accept proffered federal funds for his state.

Governors who took strong stands for or against the New Deal were rare, however, and the New Deal as a national movement had surprisingly little immediate impact upon southern politics and politicians at the state level. The majority of them apparently mildly favored what was happening in Washington— perhaps because of the predispositions of their constituencies— but few were able or willing to make the New Deal much of an issue in their states. Perhaps these politicians worried over federal infringement of states' rights. No doubt some of them were timid about expressing a definite opinion when there was no predominant trend for or against the Rooseveltian way. More likely they feared too close affiliation with an administration only partially successful in its attacks upon basic economic deficiencies.

Most of these men were usually unknown politicians who presided over relatively neutral administrations. One authority described them as "nobodies—moderate, undramatic, yawn-inspiring men with legislative programs as pedestrian as they were unsuccessful." Most state governments seemed relatively impervious to national events, and state leaders were content with that situation. Even though many ran for office on New Deal platforms, they were seldom sincere enthusiasts. Southern politicians generally accepted as much New Deal money and projects as they could wangle, but they viewed the New Deal as a way of keeping themselves in power rather than a way of liberalizing state policy. They cooperated with Roosevelt's programs but made hardly any efforts to sell them—except at election time. The overriding characteristics of southern state politics in the thirties were factionalism rather than party discipline, patronage not policy, and practicality instead of idealism.

In the long run the New Deal's greatest effect upon the southern states was a new relationship between the national and state governments. Never again would state governors or legislators act on major matters without first considering the consequences of their acts in relation to the federal government—including its regulations and its largess. They might orate about states' rights, they might grumble about federal regulations, and they might criticize specifics of the numerous federal programs; but their misgivings would not prevent them from accepting—indeed, actively seeking—federal programs and the money accompanying them.

PROLOGUE TO
DISENCHANTMENT

Southern voters had overwhelmingly supported Roosevelt for president in 1932, and their admiration continued during the New Deal era. Viewing the economic shambles around them, southerners welcomed the legislation of the early New Deal that provided for the distribution of great sums of money to millions of farmers, laid plans to help millions of unemployed workers, financed experimentation in unprecedented regional planning, pledged billions of dollars to prevent foreclosures on homes and farms, allocated huge sums for public works projects, guaranteed protection of small bank accounts, committed the nation to an unheard-of program of government-industry cooperation, and for the first time in history provided for federal regulation of Wall Street. Joining Roosevelt in office in 1933 were large Democratic majorities in Congress; most of these Democrats, southerners included, were enthusiastic supporters of Roosevelt's policies. During the First Hundred Days of the New Deal, southerners supported and voted for agricultural legislation, the emergency banking bill, the Civilian Conservation Corps, the Tennessee Valley Authority, the National Industrial Recovery Act, and a host of other measures. If a few conservative southern legislators had constitutional doubts, if some feared the passing of the Old South by such enactments or wondered about the future of states' rights, they sublimated their doubts, fears, and questions to cope with the avalanche of legislation.

In 1934 when the New Deal Congress was in its second session, many more bills were passed. They were less important than those of the Hundred Days, and the second batch of legislation proceeded at a more leisurely pace than the first rush to attack the crisis. These measures were being considered at a time when the results—not all of them good—of the earlier legislation were being tabulated. Economic conditions were improving, but not nearly as fast as optimists had hoped. More importantly, the almost unanimous support Roosevelt had received in Congress in 1933 was slowly dwindling. Clustering around a trio of southerners—Glass and Byrd of Virginia and Josiah W. Bailey of North Carolina—a group of economic conservatives began to snipe at the president and his programs. Glass had publicly raised constitutional questions about some of the Hundred Days legislation. Before the New Deal was six months old, the inflexible senator wrote that its methods "have been brutal and absolutely in contravention of every guaranty of the Constitution and of the whole spirit of sane civilization." He told Hugh Johnson, director of the National Recovery Administration, that the agency's symbol, the Blue Eagle (which he called a "blue buzzard"), was a "bird of prey" that created "a reign of terror among thousands of struggling small industries." He considered the NRA "unconstitutional . . . tyrannical and literally brutal." Of the ten major issues of 1933–34, the irascible Glass voted against six and failed to vote on a seventh. He was easily the most anti–New Deal Democrat, based on comparative voting records from 1933 to 1939. In 1934 he publicly declared that the New Deal "is not only a mistake; it is a disgrace to the Nation," and he questioned why New Dealers called themselves Democrats. "Why, Thomas Jefferson would not speak to those people," he concluded. But his fiery, aging, lonely voice was drowned in the flood of legislation.

Glass's colleague Byrd had voted for the first emergency acts, but he soon left the Roosevelt bandwagon as he "watched with much apprehension the growing tendency toward centralization of government in Washington." While he had been governor of Virginia, Byrd was a determined exponent of fiscal orthodoxy, and he carried this principle with him to the Senate. By late 1934 he was already a frequent critic of Rooseveltian programs. Like Glass and Byrd, Bailey was a strong party man, but he bridled at the New Deal's large-scale federal expenditures and at grants of power to the executive. He was more vulnerable politically than his Virginia colleagues, and he muted his opposition in public—at times he even indicated support for the administration—but privately his hostility to the New Deal was unconcealed. Bailey's economic conservatism prompted him to oppose both the AAA and the NRA. He wrote: "It is un-American to prescribe by law what a farmer may sell, a manufacturer shall make or a consumer shall pay. It denies Liberty, which is the breath of our Republic's life. There is no half-way ground. We will stick to Liberty or go over to Communism."

Glass, Byrd, Bailey, and Senators Thomas P. Gore of Oklahoma and Millard E. Tydings of Maryland were the leading conservative critics of the early New Deal. These five men have been labeled the "Democratic irreconcilables" of the Senate. None except Glass was willing to be counted as an "unreconstructed rebel," each of them admitting that many of Roosevelt's

"Two-Gun Huey"—a contemporary caricature of Huey Long. (*The Philadelphia Inquirer*)

actions were good and his motives pure. The reservations of these
men about the New Deal did not symbolize a southern movement
away from Roosevelt. The few dissenters were relatively alone in
the first New Deal days, as their colleagues and their constituents
remained enchanted with the president. The irreconcilables had
no real impact on the progress of legislation or on its nature. They
were not in step with suggested solutions for economic woes, and
they did not reflect the thinking of southern voters who overwhelmingly supported the popular president.

The most intense criticism of the early New Deal came not
from the conservative right, but from the liberal left. Louisiana's
Huey Long, now a senator, had supported Roosevelt's bid for the
presidential nomination in 1932, and he may have played a crucial
role in the behind-the-scenes jockeying at the convention. He
voted for such New Deal measures as home loans, farm relief, the
Tennessee Valley Authority, Prohibition repeal, and regulation of
the stock market. But the independent senator parted ways with
Roosevelt when he opposed the new banking laws (he filibustered
against the emergency banking proposal), NIRA, income taxes,
and governmental purchase of silver. In 1934 Long spoke frankly
on the Senate floor: "Whenever the administration has gone to the
left I have voted with it, and whenever it has gone to the right I
have voted against it."

Long presented the Roosevelt administration with a serious
threat when he unveiled his Share-Our-Wealth program, a broad,
rather nebulous, and continually altered proposal that included
confiscating the bank accounts of the wealthy and redistributing
them so that all Americans would have money in the bank.
Specifically Long suggested that all personal fortunes over $3
million be liquidated, yielding a total of $170 billion to be
deposited in the United States Treasury. This money was then to
be parceled out in $4,000 or $5,000 sums to every family in the
United States to be used for buying homes, automobiles, or
radios. All persons over sixty-five (later, sixty) years of age were to
receive pensions of $30 per month, or more if needed. The
minimum wage was to be adjusted to provide at least $2,500 a
year per worker, thus increasing the purchasing power of an
important segment of the population. The government would
regulate workers' hours, purchase and store agricultural surpluses,
and make cash payment of veterans' bonuses immediately.
Finally, Long suggested that the remainder of the confiscated
funds go to intelligent young men for college educations.

Long wildly overestimated the amount of money the government would gain from confiscation, and he underestimated the number of families who would receive it under his plan. He ignored the insurmountable problems involved in redistributing nonmonetary wealth and he showed little interest in the serious state of the nation's economy. Yet however impractical the scheme was and may seem today, it was the brainchild of a skilled political craftsman who had worked on his masterpiece for a dozen years. The program appealed to almost every segment of the American population: farmers, urbanites, the aged, underpaid and overworked laborers, veterans, and high-school graduates. Within a month of its official launching in February 1934, the Share-Our-Wealth movement had enrolled over 200,000 members, and by the end of the year the number grew to over 3,000,000. Spectacular growth continued in 1935 when people in every state joined S-O-W clubs, the total membership of which was 4,684,000. Observers professed to see the makings of a nationwide political movement directed by Long. While they were probably overreacting, Long's drive for political power cannot be discounted. Until his assassination in September 1935, he was a force that Roosevelt and his associates could not take lightly.

In June 1935, the president began to press Congress to pass five major pieces of legislation before that body recessed to escape the humidity and heat of a summer in Washington. The proposals had been introduced before, but Congress had dawdled and the administration had not applied pressure for action. Called the Second New Deal, this legislation consisted of a far-reaching labor relations proposal, a new banking bill, a public utilities holding company measure, a social security bill, and a "soak the rich" tax scheme. The last two proposals constituted Roosevelt's official response to Huey Long's Share-Our-Wealth program, and they were to some extent the president's attempt to "steal Long's thunder," to use FDR's own phrase. Before the Second Hundred Days ended, Congress passed all five pieces of legislation demanded by the president, although not without some overt opposition from the South. These acts generally stressed reform rather than relief and recovery, giving a broader dimension to the long-range implications of the New Deal; and they pointed toward permanent changes in American political institutions.

The greatest outcry against the Second New Deal measures came from the political right. Conservatives in both parties and on both sides of the Mason-Dixon Line who were unhappy with one

or more of these laws joined the "irreconcilables." The previous
cloakroom grumbling of a few southern Democrats spread to
committee meetings and to the floor of Congress when New Deal
supporters introduced the second flood of innovative legislation.
Southern conservatives protested that the Wagner labor relations
bill would encourage conflict, foster tyranny by unions, and
"re-establish medievalism in industry." The banking proposal,
whipped through the House of Representatives virtually unchanged from Roosevelt's original proposal, encountered the
determined opposition of Carter Glass in the Senate. As a firm
states' righter, Glass was alarmed by centralization of banking
control in the federal government. He opposed changes lessening
the power of private bankers, and he worked with lobbyists for
large New York banks to develop an opposing strategy. Glass
successfully amended the bill so many times that he essentially
rewrote it before it finally passed the Senate. As he boasted, "We
did not leave enough of the . . . bill with which to light a
cigarette." When the president presented one of the signature pens
to the senator, a bystander stage-whispered, "He should have
given him an eraser instead." Even with the Glass amendments,
however, the bill noticeably increased federal control of banking
and was in reality a victory for New Dealers, "dressed up as a
defeat."

Southern conservatives charged that the social security concept was a violation of traditional American values of self-help,
self-denial, and individual responsibility; but no senator from the
South voted against the bill. Byrd and Glass opposed the measure
on principle, but, recognizing the bill's popularity, they did not
vote at all. The independent Long filibustered to prevent an
appropriation for the Social Security Board, but Roosevelt
outsmarted the "Kingfish" by transferring funds from NRA and
WPA appropriations until the next session of Congress. When
Roosevelt decided to recommend the radical tax measure to
Congress, he gleefully announced to a subordinate that Pat
Harrison, the chairman of the Senate Finance Committee, was
"going to be so surprised he'll have kittens on the spot." An early
supporter of New Deal legislation, Harrison had become increasingly wary of Roosevelt's legislative suggestions. The Mississippian did all he could to slow down the progress of the bill, to
bottle it up, to amend it, and to defeat it; but by the end of the
summer social security was finally passed.

If only a few conservatives raised questions about the First

New Deal, others joined the opposition during the summer while the Second New Deal was being enacted. Even though the bills all passed with comfortable margins, the growing ranks of conservatism revealed trouble ahead for Roosevelt. Party loyalty or knowledge that their constituents were mostly pro-New Deal had kept many moderates in line, but the variety of the legislation and its long-range implications brought out heretofore unexpressed reservations. "Cotton Ed" Smith and Walter George were only two of the most vocal southern conservatives who thereafter would increase their opposition to New Deal measures, and many who remained loyal to the president, such as Robinson and Harrison, worked cautiously to rein in the "radicalism" of future New Deal programs. The 1935 session had begun with the president consistently opposed only by the five irreconcilable Democrats (and sixteen Republican conservatives). When the session ended, nineteen of the seventy Democratic senators had voted against at least two of the seven key New Deal measures enacted. A comparable situation existed in the House. Southerners made up a large part of this growing disenchantment with the New Deal. Within two years their dissatisfaction would increase to obstructionism.

Most southerners in Washington and the great majority of their constituents supported Roosevelt throughout the 1930s, however. When Roosevelt swept the country in the 1936 presidential election, southerners were among his most ardent supporters. The president lost the backing of some southern Democrats who believed he had undermined the virtues of thrift and self-reliance, that he had turned his back on goals such as equality of opportunity in favor of security and social rights, and that a group of social and economic planners controlled him. But most of the southern electorate was preoccupied with economic reality, not theory; they believed that Roosevelt was doing the job well as president. They had faith that he was solving the nation's economic problems, and specifically they were happy to receive government checks (social security benefits, farm subsidies, CCC checks) in a time of financial deprivation.

Popular opinion had little effect on the conservative minority. In the summer of 1937 a dozen conservative Democratic senators, led by southerners, openly broke with the president and were instrumental in establishing an informal, bipartisan coalition to fight him. The leader of the new bloc was Josiah Bailey, who criticized the president's failure to balance the budget and his refusal to rout sit-down strikers. Along with Bailey, who believed that he was "making a battle of Constitutional Representative Government as opposed to mass Democracy," the new alliance included George, Glass, Byrd, and South Carolina's Smith, as well as some border state and northern conservative Democrats. In combination with Republicans, this informal bloc effectively stymied further New Deal legislation. In December 1937 these men circulated a manifesto, drafted by Bailey and Republican Arthur Vandenberg of Michigan, in which they called for a balanced budget, states' rights, and other conservative principles. The manifesto was important because it crystallized opinion among dissident groups and provided a positive program for New Deal critics. In 1938 this bloc of thirty conservatives (composed almost equally of Democrats and Republicans) managed to repeal the undistributed profits tax, to reduce the capital gains tax, and to come within three votes of blocking the executive reorganization bill. The conservatives generally opposed the spread of federal power and bureaucracy, denounced deficit spending, criticized labor unions, and excoriated most welfare programs. They sought to "conserve" a pre-1933 America.

RACE, REGIONALISM, AND ROOSEVELT

Until the 1930s the Democratic party had given scant attention to black voters, assuming that their devotion to the party of the Great Emancipator was unalterable. But blacks in both North and South benefited from the New Deal programs and they began to sense that a new protector of their interests occupied the White House; despite his party label Roosevelt was their savior. He especially attracted poverty-stricken black tenants in the South and depressed blacks in the northern urban ghettos. If the New Deal did not help blacks as much as it promised, they nevertheless gained a measure of hope from the flurry of activity that the New Deal produced in their behalf. New Deal politicians came to realize that the nation's black population was ripe for Democratic appeals, and Democratic overtures and black receptiveness combined to bring about a revolution in black voting behavior that remains in American politics today.

The election of 1936 was the turning point in this historical development. Black leaders who had soured on the Republican party as early as 1932 openly supported Roosevelt in 1936, and the Democrats encouraged this change. When the votes were tallied in November, blacks had voted their economic interest—in favor of the New Deal. They cast fully 75 percent of their votes for Roosevelt, an amazing turnabout from the 1928 election, when the Democratic candidate had received no more than 25 percent of the black vote. As it developed, they changed their registrations and continued to vote Democratic in the future. Even though the majority of southern blacks were not active politically, those who did register and vote followed this pattern. The stage was set for the majority of southern blacks to adhere to the Democratic party when registration and voting barriers were lifted after the Second World War.

Southern Democrats in the early thirties raised eyebrows at the presence of blacks in the New Deal coalition and at the administration's apparent future plans for the black voter. Roosevelt began to walk a political tightwire when he included both blacks and southern conservatives in his coalition. The black man in politics had been anathema to the South's white leadership since the days of Reconstruction, and southerners in Washington expressed misgivings when party leaders continually made overtures to blacks. Roosevelt hesitated to speak out for black rights for fear of alienating southern congressmen upon whom he had to depend for leadership to pass his economic legislation. On occasion he admitted that his caution on such matters was in direct proportion to his eagerness for southern congressional support; but that caution did not allay southern misgivings. In the beginning, only a few shrewd enemies of the New Deal such as Carter Glass were prescient enough to detect the tiny ripples of the civil rights movement that would become a tidal wave in postwar America. At first arguing against the New Deal on the grounds of unconstitutionality, Glass soon charged that southern traditions were being upset by the activities of New Deal agencies. He worried over the possibility that the white supremacy tradition would also be disturbed. His concern embraced New Dealers as well as New Deal measures and agencies. Glass knew that Secretary of the Interior Harold L. Ickes had been president of the Chicago chapter of the National Association for the Advancement of Colored People, and that other New Dealers had similarly identified with black progress. When these and the more politically minded administration leaders openly courted black support after 1934, other southerners in Washington shared Glass's concern.

Several black delegates from northern states attended the 1936 Democratic national convention; when a black minister offered the invocation at the opening session, "Cotton Ed" Smith stalked out of the auditorium. Long noted for his Negrophobia, Smith's action revealed more than simply racial prejudice. He said, "I want any man, black, white, red or yellow, to pray for me, but I don't want anyone praying for me politically." If only a few southerners in Washington shared his fears about the future role of blacks in American politics, they could have been safely ignored; but racial prejudice was ingrained in all southern senators and almost every southern congressman. Southerners who had stood staunchly with Roosevelt on New Deal legislation could not tolerate the national Democratic party's overtures to blacks. Mississippi's Senator Bilbo and Representative John E. Rankin, two of the South's most unswerving New Dealers in Congress, joined opponents Glass, Byrd, and Bailey on the race question.

The presence of blacks at the 1936 convention was only one significant omen. Dominated by a coalition made up of several northern groups, the convention wiped out the century-old rule requiring the Democratic nominee to win two-thirds of the delegates' votes in order to obtain the nomination. The rule had long been a powerful weapon for southern Democrats; its rejection abolished an important political veto theretofore held by the South.

At the height of power after the election victory in 1936, the president assumed that he had a mandate from the American people to move the New Deal along a more liberal route. His attempt to "pack" the Supreme Court exemplified this goal; but by the time the battle on the Court-packing bill was over, Roosevelt found himself out of favor with a great many former supporters. Among southerners, he anticipated and received the strong opposition of Bailey and Glass, and he should not have been surprised when Byrd, George, and Smith joined them. Protests from usually reliable party regulars like John Nance Garner and Tom Connally of Texas were not anticipated, however. Race was a major factor in this violent reaction to the Court-packing plan; southerners suspected that FDR intended to use Court reform to revolutionize race relations and destroy white supremacy. They assumed that the plan was a plot to cement northern blacks within the Democratic party by appointing judges who would upset southern racial patterns. Many southern voters who wanted the Court unchanged also viewed the plan as an attack upon a bastion of white domination. A few southerners, such as Robinson, Harrison, and James Byrnes of South Carolina believed that their positions as party and Senate leaders required their loyalty. Other southern senators did not oppose the plan for the same reasons, but neither did they lend support; Hugo Black of Alabama was the only southern enthusiast. The dispute ended with an ironic twist shortly afterwards, when Roosevelt appointed Black to a vacancy on the Supreme Court; he was to become the most outspoken and consistent defender of civil rights in the Court's long history. The Court battle in itself may have been unimportant in regard to southern reaction to Roosevelt, but as southerners became increasingly critical of the president, his goals, and his party, it served as a turning point in southern political history. In the future the South would be called upon to choose between its fealty to the Democratic party and its stand on race.

The Democratic party of the 1930s was a coalition of many elements: northern city machines, organized labor, the newer immigrants, blacks, intellectuals, and southerners. During the first New Deal, these elements generally held together as the president and the party worked to rid the nation of economic stagnation. The second New Deal weakened the coalition, and by 1937 it was torn apart. A major factor in this disintegration was the gradual disenchantment of southerners in Washington with Rooseveltian programs. With only a few exceptions, southern moderate and conservative leaders were in agreement with early New Deal policies and programs. But when later programs violated southern concepts of the relationship between states and the national government, representatives of the rural south became less enthusiastic. Indeed, conservative strength grew as the decade passed, so that by 1937 and 1938 a group of southerners was able to prevent the passage of additional laws. Although the majority of the southerners in Washington and the southern populace remained loyal to Roosevelt, his program, and his party, the social changes begun during the depression—specifically in regard to blacks—had planted the seeds for southerners' future antagonism to the Democratic party.

The Great Depression, coming in the fourth decade of the twentieth century, marked the end of a long era in southern life that went back at least to the beginnings of large-scale cotton culture in the 1790s, when the cotton gin was invented. The depression's effects were soon apparent everywhere. The South had become intensely agricultural, almost defiantly so. But, dependent upon national and world economies, it was a precarious way of life. The Great Depression brought it to a crashing end.

As if the depression had not exploded one noble dream, it began to affect another—the continuing presence of a huge mass of subservient, docile blacks who would help do the South's work without too much complaining about the region's frequently poverty-level standards. The New Deal of the Rooseveltian era could not stop with economic measures, even in the relatively more comfortable North; it almost certainly had to take up social problems, which were entangled with the nation's economic (and thereby political) problems. The New Deal in its later measures began to contest the South's social arrangements. A quarter century and more would pass before this change would register in the South's politics, but the future was dimly evident by the end of the 1930s when, with the approach of a new world war in Europe, the Great Depression began to disappear.

FOUR

White
Politicians
and Black
Civil Rights

The slow rise of black Americans toward equality with whites is surely one of the major themes in the country's history during the twentieth century. At no time were southern politics of more interest in this regard than during the 1940s. At that time the nation's black populace had not yet entirely awakened from the repressions of the past, from economic degradation, social inequality, and political nonentity. Yet the social programs of the New Deal inevitably affected the lives of black people as well as whites. The Second World War, like the war of 1914–18, again offered economic opportunities and once more inspired southern blacks as well as whites to go North. In the immediate postwar years the confusions of the Democratic party after the death of Roosevelt and the appearance in the presidency of Harry S. Truman raised new possibilities for the emancipation of American blacks. Not all of them had been explored when the decade came to an end and the Truman administration prepared to leave office; but the way to equality had been cleared.

THE FIRST YEARS
OF THE 1940s

In the 1920s political issues in the South were strictly local or regional, and southern politicians had been relatively unimportant and uninfluential in national affairs. During the Great Depression of the following decade, southern politicians were still preoccupied with state and local matters, particularly those economic in nature, but economic conditions had forced them to turn to the national government for solutions. Southern senators and congressmen in Washington took on new importance during the New Deal era. By the end of that era black economic and political power had begun to grow; race, which had long dominated southern local and state politics, had become a factor at the national level by the beginning of the 1940s, and southerners drifted inexorably into the national arena.

Blacks in the United States were so degraded throughout the first third of the twentieth century that those years have been labeled "the age of segregation." Restrictions and regulations that were formalized or inaugurated at the beginning of the century prevailed in the decades that followed. Residential segregation, prohibitions in public accommodations, the lack of good job opportunities, separate and unequal educational facilities, and restricted participation in politics were common in both the North and the South. In the face of white solidarity black leaders and organizations had been unsuccessful in rectifying these conditions.

Some progress occurred when the NAACP resorted to the nation's courts in the 1930s, particularly in the desegregation of professional schools and universities. New Deal programs designed to assist the struggling American worker proved beneficial to blacks, who lay at the bottom of the heap of unemployed laborers. During the Second World War and the immediate postwar years, blacks continued to make advances as they agitated for their share of the promises of American life. Northern politicians, mindful of the inherent political benefits, helped the black population overcome major obstacles. Southern politicians did not approve of black progress, criticized northern politicians who advocated it, and resisted civil rights programs that would alter the status quo in race relations.

Having won some battles over school desegregation and experienced an increase of political power in the late thirties, blacks intensified pressures to improve their economic conditions when the Second World War began. Realizing the nation needed all the manpower it could muster during the wartime emergency, blacks knew they could contribute to and profit from the national war effort. Early in the war black leaders demanded that their people be accorded full participation in building the nation's defenses.

When new defense industries were established and old ones geared up for maximum production, blacks protested racial discrimination within them, but to no avail. To dramatize the black man's working status, in February 1941 a group of blacks led by A. Philip Randolph, a longtime racial activist and president of the Brotherhood of Sleeping Car Porters, organized the March on Washington Movement. The march was scheduled for 1 July, and one hundred thousand participants were expected. In the past President Roosevelt had essentially ignored black demands, preferring not to force the color question directly, because he needed southern congressional support for his pet legislation. But a potentially disruptive mass black demonstration in Washington could be politically harmful to a nation preparing for war, and the president could not ignore the threat. After a series of conferences between administration leaders and Randolph's group, the march was canceled when President Roosevelt agreed to issue a directive against discrimination and to establish a grievance committee. On 25 June the president issued Executive Order 8802 which forbade discrimination in defense industries and training programs, made nondiscrimination clauses in defense contracts mandatory, and established a five-man Fair Employment Practices Committee to receive and investigate complaints of discrimination and to take appropriate steps to redress valid grievances. In 1943 the president issued Executive Order 9346 extending the committee's jurisdiction and enforcement powers. The FEPC in reality had little power behind its directives, however, and it was chronically underfinanced. Although it did not recommend the cancellation of a single defense contract, the committee helped advance black employment in war industries, and it successfully encouraged federal employment services in many communities to hire blacks. Even though discrimination was still flagrant, blacks for the first time had a federal agency that was specifically interested in their problems.

Southerners in Congress who in the past had generally favored Roosevelt and his programs joined with longtime Roosevelt opponents to present a united front in regard to race. They could not prevent the issuance of executive orders, but they had the power of the purse, which they exercised without compunction. The temporary FEPC struggled for funds, supported during the first two years of its life from the president's limited emergency fund and thereafter from niggardly legislative appropriations. In 1944 a Senate subcommittee dominated by southerners voted to delete money for the FEPC from the war agencies appropriations bill, but the full committee restored the funds. Senators Bilbo, Richard Russell, and Walter George fulminated against the committee's action, but despite (or because of) southern arguments and objections, the Senate voted to sustain the appropriation of $500,000, although Russell had successfully included certain restrictive amendments to Executive Order 9346. In 1945 the committee's appropriation was cut to $250,000 after a tremendous parliamentary struggle that almost killed several emergency agencies included in that year's war agencies appropriation bill. Southerners gave notice that they would approve no other appropriation for the FEPC, and even the approved sum did not permit the wartime committee to exist for the entire fiscal year. The temporary FEPC expired in 1946 for lack of funds.

In the meantime, advocates of minority rights had introduced legislation to establish a permanent Fair Employment Practices Commission. An FEPC bill was introduced in the House in 1942, but southerners prevented it from reaching the House floor. In January 1945 thirteen House bills and one Senate bill were introduced. Again the bills were bottled up in southern-controlled committees. At one time Florida's Senator Claude Pepper had suggested the possibility of a compromise on a permanent FEPC but later he announced his decision to fight it; the liberal Pepper had received enough mail on the subject to make him more sensitive to traditional southern sentiment. Southerners carried on a twenty-three-day filibuster to prevent the Senate from considering one of the FEPC bills, ending when both sides agreed to vote on a cloture petition to limit debate. Even though the war itself demanded prime attention from the entire nation, whites in the South could not forget their prejudices toward blacks. They were concerned about the black's future competitive role in the economic structure of the nation, and they were not eager to see the black man break out of the economic bonds that had held him down for generations. When the black man began to make more of an issue of his lowly economic status and when some prospects for advancement appeared, southern concern increased. To a man southern politicians in Washington catered to these fears and prejudices.

Farm Security Administration photograph. Library of Congress.

Preoccupation with the black was evident in the controversy over the soldier vote issue. When it was suggested that arrangement be made for voting-age soldiers to cast ballots in elections at home, all congressmen and senators responded favorably; nothing could have been more politically inexpedient than for an elected official to suggest that young men overseas fighting for the survival of democracy should not exercise the right of franchise. Most states provided for absentee ballots, but the process of securing them was always cumbersome and often lengthy, and it was particularly inconvenient for the overseas soldier. Suggestions for a soldier ballot developed in the early days of the war, but controversy arising from political self-interest over the kind of ballot to be approved caused Congress to spend an inordinate amount of time on the subject, delaying a decision until 1944.

The partisan blocs in Congress generally divided into three groups on the issue: northern Democrats desired a federal ballot, which would facilitate soldiers voting in presidential elections; Republicans were inclined to favor a state ballot, which afforded soldiers greater opportunity to vote for state officials as well as presidential candidates; southern Democrats also opted for a state ballot so that the states could continue to control the standards of residence, registration, and voter eligibility. Early progress in the outlawing of discriminatory white primaries had received a setback when the Supreme Court in *Grovey* v. *Townsend* (1935) ruled that action taken by the Texas Democratic party to exclude whites from the party's primaries did not constitute state violation of the equal protection clause of the Constitution. In the late thirties and early forties each of the southern states still had a maze of exclusionary voting requirements for blacks so that only a few could vote in southern elections. The politicians did not want this tradition broken on foreign battlefields. When the administration suggested waiving the poll tax for soldiers, southerners objected violently because they feared that the removal of the tax for soldiers would be used as an argument for its removal for blacks. Southerners associated states' rights and poll taxes with limited numbers of black voters. As the election of 1944 approached, Republicans and southerners formed a coalition to push through Congress a bill providing for state-controlled ballots. Republicans had come to believe that the waiving of state restrictions would benefit the Democratic presidential candidate; southerners continued to be obsessed with the specter of the black voter.

Although other devices overshadowed the poll tax, every southern state had instituted this requirement between 1890 and 1908. North Carolina had repealed its poll tax in 1920, and Louisiana and Florida had followed in 1934 and 1937 respectively—during the New Deal era, when reforms had stimulated national interest in poll tax repeal, even though studies showed that repeal had not resulted in increased black voting. In 1938 President Roosevelt declared in a press conference that the tax was an outmoded instrument for restricting the suffrage, further stimulating reformers' attempts to abolish it. Beginning in 1939 bills were introduced into every wartime Congress to eliminate the poll tax as a voting requirement in national elections. In 1941 Senator Pepper introduced a bill that would make it unlawful to require the tax in connection with any election for national offices, since the levy was not a constitutional qualification for voters. Pepper's bill applied to both primary and general elections, and its format was the model for future anti–poll tax legislation. After the House passed a bill in September 1942, Tom Connally of Texas and Kenneth McKellar of Tennessee led a senatorial filibuster against it. Connally directed the parliamentary strategy but Bilbo carried the chief burden in the oratorical marathon. The filibuster lasted a full week, dominated by the "bilbonic plague." As one observer noted, "Substituting shibboleths for statesmanship, he [Bilbo] has hidden behind the verbiage of States Rights, White Supremacy, and Democratic Solidarity." An attempt to apply cloture failed because many senators, even though they favored the anti–poll tax measure, hesitated to apply a rule that in the future might be used against them.

Other anti–poll tax bills were introduced in the remaining wartime Congresses; one passed in the House in May 1943, but another Senate filibuster killed it. On this occasion Connally, rather than the unpopular Bilbo, led the opposition forces. In 1943 Pepper introduced a resolution to tighten the Senate rules on debate and to make cloture easier to invoke. These changes would help an anti–poll tax law's chances, but no one heeded the suggestion. The issue came up again in the Senate in May 1944, at which time southerners spoke without restraint. Just before the filibuster Bilbo told the Mississippi state legislature: "The poll tax brings the entire race question before the American people. . . . It has become necessary for us now to consider and to openly discuss the forces which are today attempting to destroy the color line. . . . We will tell our negro-loving, Yankee friends to 'Go Straight to Hell.' " On the Senate floor he talked of race relations, states' rights, and federal bureaucracy. Once again the Senate failed to vote cloture, and the anti–poll tax supporters capitulated. The House passed another anti–poll tax bill in 1945, but the Senate refused to take it up until July 1946, at which time Majority Leader Alben Barkley invoked cloture immediately, before a filibuster could develop. The cloture vote fell short of a two-thirds majority again, and the Senate did not consider the measure. Throughout the wartime debates on the poll tax, southern senators except for Pepper were unanimous in their opinions, and southern House members were nearly so. The issue remained and was a part of the larger controversy in the postwar era concerning the role of the black man in America.

A NEW PRESIDENT

When Harry S. Truman became president in April 1945, he brought to the White House a mixed background in regard to black civil rights. Truman apparently possessed white racist attitudes that were common in the border state of Missouri when he first became involved in politics there; but despite his inclinations he recognized the potential power of the black vote while he was a member of the Pendergast machine in Kansas City. Concentrated in Kansas City and St. Louis, some one hundred thirty thousand black voters began to have political influence in Missouri about the time Truman started his political career. He was careful to cultivate these black voters, and they played a role in his successful statewide senatorial campaign in 1934. When he decided to run for reelection in 1940, his chances of winning even the primary race appeared slim; the Pendergast machine no longer dominated Kansas City, and President Roosevelt privately supported the senator's opponent. Truman campaigned vigorously, however, making special appeals to blacks, whose votes in St. Louis constituted his margin of victory in the Democratic primary and made up a significant percentage of his victorious totals in the close general election.

Remembering the source of his victory, Truman molded a somewhat problack civil rights record after he appeared in the United States Senate. He took a reasonably active interest in civil rights legislation, and he was counted among the liberals whenever such bills were introduced. Truman seemed to favor the 1938 antilynching bill, although a southern filibuster prevented a vote. He joined with northern liberals who signed cloture petitions and endorsed motions to close debate on the antilynching bill, actions that indicated that the Missourian would have voted for the bill itself had he been given the chance. In conversation with a southern senator, Truman made a revealing remark: "You know I am against this [antilynching] bill, but if it comes to a vote, I'll have to vote for it. All my sympathies are with you but the Negro vote in Kansas City and St. Louis is too important." Two years later he voted for an amendment to the Selective Service Act to prevent discrimination against members of minority groups who desired to volunteer to serve in the army. As chairman of the Senate Special Committee to investigate the National Defense Program during his second Senate term, Truman directed his attention to waste, inefficiency, and corruption among defense contractors, as well as to many other phases of the war effort. In this capacity he presided over hearings on alleged racial discrimination by companies holding government contracts, but little was accomplished and the Truman Committee was accused of not taking this subject seriously. During the war years Truman gave his total support to all proposals to finance the Fair Employment Practices Committee. Furthermore, he sponsored legislation to award a combat command to Benjamin Davis, the army's first black general; he voted for cloture to end a 1942 poll tax filibuster; and he spoke in favor of an investigation into the relationship of segregation and opportunities for blacks in the armed forces. In the midst of these problack votes and words, Truman voted against an anti–poll tax amendment to the soldier vote bill. He never explained why he supported the southern position, but perhaps his personal sympathies for the southern point of view overrode political considerations. Missouri was not a poll tax state, and Truman possibly felt that he had little to lose politically by voting as he did.

Roosevelt's selection of Truman for second place on the 1944 national Democratic ticket was no accident. Truman was a political moderate on all subjects, including race relations. South Carolina's James Byrnes, clearly identified with southern racism, was unacceptable to liberal Democrats, just as the freewheeling liberal Henry Wallace was anathema to the conservatives. Without doubt Wallace's convention speech in which he spoke out for racial justice, economic democracy, equal education opportunities, and the abolition of the poll tax was an important factor in his defeat for renomination. Truman was highly acceptable to the South, but Wallace had captured the imagination of black convention delegates who were disappointed and skeptical when Truman was nominated. Aware of this reaction when he was interviewed by the *Pittsburgh Courier*, an influential black newspaper, Truman said: "I have always been for equality of opportunity in work, working conditions and political rights. I think the Negro in the armed forces ought to have the same treatment and opportunities as every other member of the armed forces. . . . I have a record for fair play toward my Negro fellow citizens that will stand examination." When he was asked about Wallace's views on civil rights, Truman replied that "no honest American can disagree with Henry Wallace. What he said [in his convention speech] was gospel."

Despite these ingratiating remarks, black leaders did not respond favorably to the Truman candidacy. Southern politicians did not help matters when they praised Truman as being "safe on states rights and the right of the state to control qualifications of its electors." Republicans attempted to hang a pro–Ku Klux Klan label on Truman, and in Harlem they told voters that "Roosevelt is old and may die and you will then have a KKK man in the White House." Even though most black leaders were less than enthusiastic about the Roosevelt-Truman ticket and the Democratic platform's token civil rights plank, they voted Democratic as did hundreds of thousands of blacks who were responsible for eight northern states falling into the Democratic column.

A few days after Truman was thrust into the presidency, Senator Olin Johnston of South Carolina wrote to the new president: "I think that your policies will be far enough to the right and not too far to the left. This in my opinion will be most valuable in securing the fullest and best cooperation of the people and the Congress." Truman soon dashed these hopes. Having had experience with the power of the black vote in Missouri and aware of the rising importance of that group in national politics, he was determined to solidify the northern black vote as soon as he became president. In the thirties and early forties, Roosevelt had catered to southern politicians at the expense of the black voter, since he believed his New Deal and wartime programs depended upon the former's influence and numerical support. As black political influence grew—particularly after the March on Washington Movement revealed how potent it could be—and as black awareness during the wartime emergency stimulated additional political activity, Rooseveltian slowness in regard to civil rights could no longer be tolerated. After the war the atmosphere and conditions were right for the Democrats to make a concerted effort to appeal to blacks. Ignoring Roosevelt's example, Truman concluded that the Democratic party needed the rising totals of northern black votes more than it needed white votes from the conservative South. Throughout his years in the presidency, Truman deliberately and calculatedly took actions to win moderate civil rights advances for blacks and at the same time to win their votes.

Less than two months after taking the presidential oath, Truman wrote to Illinois Congressman Adolph Sabath, chairman of the House Rules Committee, urging that committee to allow the House to vote upon a long-pending bill providing for a permanent

Fair Employment Practices Commission. He also protested recent action by the House Appropriations Committee cutting off funds for the continuation of the wartime FEPC. By writing this letter in which he stated that it was un-American to discriminate in employment because of race, creed, or color, Truman took his first stand as president regarding the basic civil rights of all Americans, and he continued to speak for a fair employment act and other civil rights legislation throughout his eight years in office. A few days after Truman's letter to Sabath was made public, Representative Frank W. Boykin of Alabama wrote the president that after a caucus, 103 House Democrats had authorized him to request a meeting with Truman "to give you our view of this terrible thing [the FEPC] that is not only tearing our Party to pieces, but the entire nation." Truman refused to receive the delegation. Southerners in Congress killed the temporary FEPC, which had operated with limited congressional approval since 1943, when they permitted the committee a small amount of money but stipulated that "in no case shall this fund be available for expenditure beyond June 30, 1946." The prospects for a renewed appropriation were nil.

Despite the death of the wartime FEPC, Truman delivered a comprehensive postwar message to Congress in September 1945 in which he suggested twenty-one guidelines for action on pressing social and economic matters, one of his recommendations being that the FEPC be made permanent. In January 1946 the president delivered a radio address to the nation, discussing certain "grave problems" that Congress was not handling adequately. He specifically mentioned the FEPC and recalled that "a small handful of Congressmen in the Rules Committee of the House" had prevented an FEPC bill from being brought to a vote. Two weeks later in his State of the Union message, he referred again to the desirability of a permanent FEPC.

When a bill to establish such a commission was brought before the Senate just after this speech, southerners responded with another filibuster. Bilbo insisted that the FEPC was "nothing but a plot to put niggers to work next to your daughters and to run your business with niggers." He reported hearing of a petition circulated in Georgia favoring the FEPC, and he assumed that "the great majority of these petitioners, representing Negroes, Quislings of the white race, and other racial minorities, hail from the city of Atlanta, the hotbed of Southern Negro intelligentsia, Communists, pinks, Reds, and other off-brands of American

Pickets opposing the FEPC filibuster in 1946. (Wide World Photos)

citizenship in the South." Senator James O. Eastland announced
that if the bill became law he would recommend to his state's
legislature that it protect the sovereignty of Mississippi by passing
a nullification proclamation. Eastland reminded the Senate that
the FEPC was sponsored by the CIO, "a carpetbag organization
that has come into the South and is attempting to destroy
Southern institutions and Southern civilization." John McClellan
of Arkansas called the bill "pernicious," and John H. Bankhead of
Alabama said it reflected the philosophy of "the Bolshevik
crowd." Senator George warned, "If this is all that Harry Truman
has to offer, God help the Democratic Party in 1946 and 1948."
After three weeks of filibustering, the Senate leadership gave up,
removed the item from the agenda, and moved on to other
matters.

On a number of occasions during the next few months
Truman spoke out for FEPC, but he apparently rarely placed
pressure directly on Congress to act. Even though he was moving
in the direction of more civil rights for blacks and more black
votes for the Democratic party, Truman tried not to deliberately
antagonize the southern bloc during his first year as president. But
southern Democrats were unhappy with him for taking a public
stand in favor of FEPC, and black leaders were critical because he
did not fulfill his promises.

Throughout 1946 the president continued to speak out for the
principle of equal justice under the law, but he was reluctant to
force the issue in Congress. In September he told an Urban
League convention in St. Louis that "if the civil rights of even one
citizen are abused, government has failed to discharge one of its
primary responsibilities"; at the same time he refused to apply
pressure for an antilynching law because, as he said, the political
timing was wrong. Black leaders encouraged their followers to
vote Republican in the midterm elections of November 1946,
because of the "southernness" of the Truman administration and
because the president had taken no effective action in their behalf.
While many other factors were responsible for the landslide
victory of the Republicans in November, black disaffection with
Truman must not be discounted. Black spokesmen were happy
with the results because the Eightieth Congress would be organized by Republicans, removing southern Democrats from pivotal
committee chairmanships from which they had stifled civil rights
legislation.

The racial question was the overriding issue in many state and local elections in the South in 1946. The gubernatorial campaign in Georgia, won by racist Eugene Talmadge, was fought entirely over the question of white supremacy. Bilbo was renominated and reelected after a campaign supercharged with racial hatred. When the Senate met in December 1946, before anyone could be sworn in, Idaho Democrat Glen H. Taylor moved that Bilbo be denied his seat, because of his unbecoming words and behavior in the Mississippi primary campaign. Southern senators rallied to their colleague's defense. The most ardent supporters were Louisiana's John Overton and Allen Ellender, the latter remarking that "Northern organizations" were behind the move to oust the Mississippian. Ellender declared, "The march is on to destroy Southern traditions which are so deeply rooted as the giants of the forest." A showdown was avoided when Senator Barkley arranged a truce after Bilbo became ill and had to enter a hospital for an operation; he died in August 1947. Even though Bilbo did not return to the Senate, forestalling a continuation of the fight to unseat him, the controversy served to publicize and dramatize division in Democratic ranks.

In January 1947 Truman delivered his State of the Union message in which he referred to racial conflict and declared that "the will to fight these crimes should be in the heart of every one of us." In his economic message to Congress two days later, the president called upon the legislators to enact a permanent FEPC. In June Truman delivered an address to an NAACP rally in front of the Lincoln Memorial in which he forthrightly spoke in favor of civil rights. Southern politicians were remarkably quiescent after this landmark speech, the first public address by an American president in the twentieth century on the question of racial discrimination. They may have assumed the president was insincere, even though after the speech Truman said to Walter White, "I mean every word of it—and I am going to prove that I do mean it."

In December 1946 Truman had taken action which he had been contemplating for several months: he issued Executive Order 9008 creating the President's Committee on Civil Rights. Authorized to recommend how civil rights might be strengthened and improved, this prestigious committee was composed of fifteen prominent Americans, including three southerners: Dr. Frank Graham, president of the University of North Carolina; Dr. Channing Tobias, director of the Phelps-Stokes education fund; and Mrs. M. E. Tilly, an Atlantan who was an official of the

Methodist Women's Society of Christian Service. There were two blacks on the committee: Tobias and Mrs. Sadie T. Alexander, a Philadelphia lawyer who was on the board of directors of the National Urban League. In his memoirs, Truman wrote that he had established this committee because postwar racial tension had manifested itself in a number of ugly incidents resulting in the loss of life. This was undoubtedly true; but political reality and black leaders' pressure for action were probably more important factors.

In October 1947 the committee issued its formal report in which it declared that the time had come to create a permanent nationwide system of guardianship for the civil rights of all Americans. Published under the title *To Secure These Rights*, the widely publicized and widely distributed report listed thirty-five specific recommendations for improving and protecting the civil rights of American citizens. Until this report was filed, President Truman had tried to satisfy black demands with rhetoric, at the same time appealing to his southern supporters by not pressing for action on civil rights. He had walked this political tightwire relatively successfully since taking office in April 1945, although he had found this increasingly difficult as time passed. Now Truman could no longer verbally support civil rights while failing to act. He could cast his lot with the advocates of black rights by pressing for legislation, or he could ignore the committee report and side with the South. The time had come for the president of the United States to make an unequivocal decision. The stand he was to take had profound impact upon the civil rights movement, the Democratic party, and the role of the South in the political history of the nation.

THE DIXIECRATS

Harry Truman was compelled to take the side of civil rights advocates in the presidential election year of 1948. First, in the midst of a cold war, Truman realized that Russian propaganda about American racial tension had to be countered if the United States' image in the United Nations and throughout the world was to be protected from permanent damage. The nation's treatment of its largest and most visible minority population might become a factor in the decisions lesser nations would make to support either the United States or Russia as the two giants globally sparred with each other. Second, in December 1947 Henry Wallace announced his intention to run for the presidency in 1948 as the candidate of his recently organized Progressive party. One of Wallace's principal policies was support of civil rights, and black voters were again attracted to this outspoken opponent of segregation and discrimination. Whatever other issues would be raised as the election approached, Wallace's candidacy guaranteed that civil rights would be included. Third, postwar events on the domestic scene, including racial tension and black calls for a full share in the promise of American life, demanded attention to the subject of race. Fourth, Truman believed the black vote could be the margin of victory in the November elections.

In view of these factors and convinced that the South would vote Democratic in November under any circumstances, Truman in February 1948 sent a special message to Congress in which he demanded action on ten recommendations of the President's Civil Rights Committee. The four proposals most directly affecting the South included a permanent FEPC, an antilynching law, an anti–poll tax measure, and the prohibition of discrimination in interstate transportation facilities. A few days before the president delivered his message, Henry Wallace had announced a program that included the first three of these proposals. Mississippi's Governor Fielding J. Wright had reacted immediately to the Wallace pronouncement by stating that he would not permit any federal action "aimed to wreck the South and its institutions." After attacking the report of the President's Committee on Civil Rights, he concluded, "Vital principles and eternal truths transcend party lines, and the day is now at hand when determined action must be taken." The Mississippi state legislature then approved a resolution supporting the governor's scarcely veiled threat of a withdrawal from the Democratic party if civil rights legislation were pressed.

Southern reaction in Washington to the president's suggestions was equally immediate and ominous. Senator Byrd asserted that the president's civil rights program constituted a "devastating broadside at the dignity of Southern traditions and institutions" and that its passage might lead to bloodshed in the South. Representative Ed Lee Gossett of Texas said the president was "kissing the feet of the minorities." Representative John Bell Williams of Mississippi claimed that southern Democrats were responsible for Truman (instead of Henry Wallace) being in the White House and that they were the best friends Truman and the Democratic party had. Williams considered Truman's speech "a mighty poor way for him to evince his gratitude." He concluded that the president "has seen fit to run a political dagger into our backs and now he is trying to drink our blood." Many southern members of Congress accused Truman of playing to the northern black vote in view of the forthcoming presidential election in November, and hints of a southern revolt in the 1948 election were made in both the House and the Senate within hours of the delivery of Truman's message. Mississippi Congressman John Rankin said the South should choose independent electors to "stop these smearing Communists who creep into every bureau and every commission that is appointed and attempt to undermine and destroy everything our people have fought for and everything we hold dear." John Overton asked southern Democrats to vote Republican or to boycott the national Democratic ticket. Eastland accused the president of attempting "to mongrelize the South," and he called upon the region to withhold its electoral votes from the Democratic party's candidate and cast them instead for a "distinguished Southerner."

Reflecting the public opinion of the region, southern newspapers had generally criticized the report of the President's Committee on Civil Rights when it was made public in October 1947. One had indicated that the committee "proposed to extinguish a smouldering and slowly dying fire by drenching it with gasoline." Many expressed similar attitudes toward Truman's speech of 2 February, some of them pleading that the president should let the states and local communities handle racial problems. The *Nashville Banner* referred to those "vicious planks" in Truman's proposed program which included "the monstrous character of an FEPC proposal, and attendant force bills transgressing both the letter and the spirit of the Constitution." It continued, "The people of the South are tired of being pushed around, subjected to abuse, invaded by a constant influx of odd characters bent on reforming it to suit their own designs of reconstruction."

Soon after the president's February 1948 address, thousands of letters, telegrams, petitions, resolutions, and other forms of protests from the South poured into the White House mail room. The mid-twentieth-century generation resurrected hundred-year-old arguments to bolster their points of view. According to the writers of these letters, Truman's suggestions were Communistic, unconstitutional, in violation of states' rights, and would result in an undesirable mongrelization of the white race. Some accused Truman of being politically motivated in his message to Congress. More than one argued that Truman did not understand the situation in the South, that southerners treated blacks well, and that conditions in the region had been misrepresented. Secession or civil war was threatened by the more aroused southerners, while others predicted that Truman's stand would provoke the revival of the Ku Klux Klan. "You have advocated and asked Congress for a lot of good legislation, both Domestic and Foreign," acknowledged one southerner, " 'but' [sic] when you asked Congress to pass your Civil Rights Legislation, and press down the Crown of Thorns on the South's brow and crucify the South's people on a Communistic Cross disguised in Negro equality, that was the straw that broke the Camel's back." Another southerner suggested in his letter to the president that if attempted enforcement followed any civil rights measures passed by Congress, "there will be enough blood shed to make the Mississippi River run RED." He then tried to appeal to Truman's conscience: "If you have the power to prevent such legislation and don't use it, you will be just as guilty of MURDER as if you had slain thousands of innocent people with your own hand."

Shortly after the president's special message on civil rights, a regular meeting of the Southern Governors Conference met in Wakulla Springs, Florida. Governors Wright of Mississippi and James Folsom of Alabama introduced a resolution calling for a special meeting of the group in Jackson, Mississippi, on 1 March "to formulate plans for activity and adopt a course of action." Most of the governors were predictably displeased with Truman's civil rights policy, but they were not prepared to bolt the sacrosanct party. Rather than endorsing the Wright-Folsom resolution, the conference appointed a five-man committee chaired by South Carolina's Governor Strom Thurmond to attempt to effect a compromise with the president. Two days after this decision, the White House announced that "there will be absolutely no compromise on any point," and at a news conference Truman declared that he would not discuss the subject with any southern group. Shortly thereafter, fifty-two southerners in the House formally condemned the civil rights message and endorsed the governors' resolution. Led by William Colmer of Mississippi, these southerners warned Truman that the Democratic party would face "serious consequences" if it included a civil rights plank in the national platform. Twenty-one southern senators pledged to "stand guard" and prevent the enactment of any civil rights measure.

Southern response to Truman's 2 February speech was more

than a "tempest in a teapot"—it was "a solid front put up for political purposes." Several southern congressmen were deadly serious about a political revolt. Before the end of February Truman unofficially launched his candidacy for reelection, confidently expecting southern resistance to fade away, as it had done in the past at election time. Truman reasoned that his overt appeals to blacks would not drive loyal southern Democrats out of his party; but even if he misgauged southern response, he believed that politically it was more expedient to win the support of the rapidly rising northern black vote than to retain white southern votes. In the past, Democratic presidential candidates had not dared risk southern opposition; by 1948 failure to attract northern black numbers was a greater risk. The political balance of power was tipping, and soon southerners would be less powerful in Washington and in Democratic party politics.

Although Truman refused to meet with the Thurmond committee, Senator J. Howard McGrath, chairman of the Democratic National Committee, did so. He attempted to pacify the southerners by stressing the moderation in Truman's stance, but he would not compromise the principles set forth by the president. After the meeting with McGrath, the committee declared that it was

"THE NEW MASON-DIXON LINE?"

Copyright 1948 *The Los Angeles Times*. Reprinted by permission.

"opposed to centralized government invading the rights of the people and the rights of the respective states" and that "the present leadership of the Democratic Party will soon realize that the South is no longer 'in the bag.' " After the committee reported that its overtures to McGrath had been unsuccessful, seven of the southern governors at a special meeting adopted a resolution specifically requesting that southern delegates to the Democratic National Convention be instructed to oppose Truman's nomination and recommending that all southern state Democratic conventions pledge their presidential electors to vote against any candidate in the November elections who favored civil rights legislation. Furthermore, they suggested that the Democratic party reinstitute a two-thirds majority for nominating a presidential candidate at the forthcoming convention (a requirement that had been dropped in 1936).

These developments divided leaders and local Democratic party organizations in the southern states. Governor R. Gregg Cherry of North Carolina announced that he would support Truman and the Democratic party under any circumstances, despite the growing hostility toward the president on the part of a vocal minority of politicians in his state. Most state and local leaders hoped to maneuver within the party framework to express their dissatisfaction with Truman and his civil rights stand, and they were too deeply imbued with Democratic loyalty to leave the party, even over such an emotional issue as black rights.

Other Democrats were willing to break with the party if it ignored their stand on the subject, however. Alabama's delegates to the forthcoming national convention were pledged to vote against any presidential aspirant who favored civil rights, and some members of the delegation publicly announced that they would withdraw from the national convention if it accepted a strong pro–civil rights statement. The Mississippi Democratic executive committee meeting in Jackson in February resolved that Mississippi's presidential electors and delegates to the national convention should vote against any candidate who favored the president's proposals. They also instructed the delegates to walk out of the convention if they were dissatisfied with the civil rights plank in the national platform. The committee then invited "all true white Jeffersonian Democrats" to meet in Jackson in May to deal on a regional basis with the trend of the national party. At this meeting, dominated by delegations from Mississippi and South Carolina, resolutions were passed urging all southern states to select delegates to the forthcoming convention who were pledged against any candidate favoring civil rights legislation. This group agreed to meet again in Birmingham after the national convention if the national party supported a strong civil rights program. Truman recognized that the southern Democrats were serious. At a news conference he implied that he would not push for civil rights legislation, and to Congressman Rankin he hinted that he was willing to compromise on a civil rights plank in the national platform. His comments were designed to hold the southerners in line, but they endangered Truman's support from northern white liberals and blacks.

In July Truman established by Executive Order 9981 the Committee on Equality of Treatment and Opportunity in the Armed Forces, later known as the Fahy Committee, after its chairman Charles H. Fahy. The seven-member group took seriously Truman's request for "concrete results"; it not only investigated conditions in the armed services, but it also helped the three military branches establish racial policies that the committee considered acceptable. After less than two years of existence, the committee brought about policies in the army, navy, and air force that were little short of revolutionary, even though they were not all put into effect immediately nor always followed in practice. The initial steps had been taken, and blacks in the future would serve in desegregated military services. Truman was playing politics with the black vote in timing the announcement of the committee's formation, since the 1948 Democratic convention was imminent. Senator Russell, an outspoken minority member of the Senate Armed Services Committee, believed that the order amounted to "unconditional surrender to the Wallace [presidential] convention, and [capitulation] to the treasonable civil disobedience campaign organized by . . . Negroes. . . ." The stage was set for conflict at the forthcoming convention.

At the Democratic national convention in Philadelphia, the platform committee approved a moderate statement expressing Truman's position. Die-hard southerners were not appeased, and northern liberals were unhappy with the seemingly equivocal language. After the committee made its majority recommendations to the convention, southern committee members presented minority resolutions. Former Governor Dan Moody of Texas offered a states' rights resolution which the convention defeated by a vote of 309 yeas to 925 nays; delegates from outside the South cast only eleven votes for this resolution. Northern liberals, led by Minneapolis's Mayor Hubert H. Humphrey, also suggested a substitute for the platform committee's recommendation in which they praised President Truman for his "courageous stand on the issue of civil rights" and urged Congress to pass civil rights laws that would prevent discrimination in voting and employment and would protect the civil liberties of all Americans. Even though the liberals praised Truman, administration leaders tried to dissociate themselves from this liberal plank for fear of forever alienating the southern white vote. Their efforts to defeat the substitute failed as the convention adopted the liberal plank by a vote of 651½ to 582½, mainly because local politicians in the big-city states needed black votes and they feared defeat if they offended the blacks. In response to the convention's action, all of Mississippi's delegates and about half of those from Alabama—a total of thirty-five—walked out as a band played "Dixie." Other southerners refused to leave the convention, but in the balloting they supported Russell of Georgia instead of Truman. Of the 276 southern delegates who remained after the walkout, 263 voted for Russell and 13 (all from North Carolina) voted for Truman. Russell later said he had allowed his nomination "only as a protest against the outrageous violations of states' rights." Truman easily won the nomination with 947½ votes. Senator Barkley of Kentucky, a border state moderate, was nominated for the vice-presidency, a move designed to appease the South, but his support of the party platform identified him with the national party, not with the South.

On 17 July, two days after the adjournment of the national convention, the disgruntled southerners convened at Birmingham as planned, where they expressed the view that the Democratic party was antisouthern and disinterested in the South's traditional stands on such matters as states' rights and the role of blacks in American society. This group of southern conservatives formed the States' Rights party; its members were later called Dixiecrats. The major leaders of this dissident southern faction were Governors Thurmond and Wright. Surprising no one, these men were unanimously nominated as the presidential and vice-presidential candidates for the new party to run on a platform decrying federal interference in state affairs.

The Dixiecrats had no hopes of winning the election. Their strategy was to take enough votes away from Truman so that neither he nor his Republican opponent could win a majority in the electoral college. If they could capture the 136 electoral votes of the eleven southern states, they would most likely forestall either major candidate from obtaining the 266 votes necessary for a clear-cut victory. Depending on the distribution of electoral votes in states outside the South, the Dixiecrats reasoned that their scheme had a good chance to work if they could control about one-half of the South's votes. With the election thrown into the House of Representatives, where each state delegation would have one vote, the southerners would hold a bargaining position strong enough to force the Democrats to promise support for southern demands. If the Democrats would not cooperate, the Dixiecrats would not hesitate to bargain with the Republicans. Eastland reasoned that Thurmond even had a chance as a compromise candidate in the House: "Northern Democrats would still prefer a Southern Democrat to a Republican, and Republicans would prefer a Southern Democrat to a Northern one." It was a grand and ambitious scheme with just enough potential to intrigue many southerners.

Since Henry Wallace remained in the presidential race, Truman now had competition from both the right and the left. The Republican candidate, New York's Governor Thomas E. Dewey, had a creditable record on civil rights and the GOP's platform was worded in such a way as to try to attract black votes. Truman had not been a popular president, and his chances of successful reelection appeared slim. After the nominating conventions were over and after the Republicans had come out for a moderate civil rights program, he called the Congress into special session to deal with a number of pressing problems, including civil rights. This move was designed to put the Republicans on the spot, for they could hardly campaign for black votes at the same time a Republican-dominated Congress was in session refusing to pass civil rights legislation. The House voted 290 to 112 for an anti–poll tax bill, but a southern filibuster prevented progress in the Senate. When the special session of Congress ended on 7 August, it had accomplished little. This failure to pass constructive legislation gave Truman his most compelling issue in the election campaign: he unmercifully hammered at the "do-nothing" Eightieth Congress. As he attacked this Republican-controlled Congress, however, he failed to mention the role southern Democrats played in stifling civil rights legislation.

As the campaign progressed, Truman made noticeable headway among black voters. The Dixiecrat rebellion had convinced blacks that Truman was a sincere advocate of their civil rights, and late in the campaign Truman made some strong statements in favor of black rights while visiting northern cities such as Cleveland, Chicago, Philadelphia, and Harlem (voters in the latter having never before been addressed in person by a president). Truman muted his advocacy of civil rights in the border states, fearing that too strong a stand there would harm his appeal to moderate white voters.

The emergence of the Dixiecrats forced Democrats in the South to make a difficult choice. The Dixiecrats appealed to southerners by arguing that they were "true Democrats," but they did not convince those who considered party regularity the highest of the political gods. Democrats whose priorities were states' rights and opposition to civil rights bolted to the Dixiecrats, but their numbers were not great. Pre-election surveys revealed that the Dixiecrats had significant strength only in South Carolina, Alabama, Mississippi, and Louisiana. There were few anti-Truman Democrats in the remainder of the South. A few days before the election Senator Russell endorsed Truman, and the chairman of the Democratic state committee of North Carolina pointed out that from the southern point of view Dewey had a less desirable record on civil rights than Truman. He asked, "What can we accomplish [by refusing to vote for Truman]?"

Every poll had predicted that Dewey would overwhelm Truman, but on election day Truman won over his three opponents, as he captured millions of votes of rural and urban dwellers, labor and the intellectuals, whites and blacks. In the electoral college he received 303 votes to Dewey's 189, Thurmond's 39, and Wallace's zero. A postelection survey revealed that 69 percent of all black votes in twenty-seven major cities had been cast for Truman. More importantly, Truman barely won the populous states of California, Illinois, and Ohio, and if considerable numbers of blacks in those states had voted for Dewey or Wallace instead of Truman, Dewey would have been elected president or the election would have been sent to the House of Representatives. Dewey had lost northern black votes by actively soliciting southern votes, but southerners did not respond to his appeals. Truman had capitalized on his civil rights proposals, while Dewey essentially remained silent about his own civil rights accomplishments. To gain northern support Truman had made several shrewd political moves; Dewey had made fatal ones. Truman also won majorities in seven southern states and several border states, where black populations were smaller and their votes not crucial but where white Democrats refused to renounce their party in the polling booth.

The Dixiecrats won the electoral votes only of South Carolina, Alabama, Mississippi, and Louisiana, plus another one from an independent-minded elector in Tennessee. If they had somehow won the votes of the other seven southern states, their designs would have been accomplished easily. Had the vote been rearranged slightly, the South would have held the powerful bargaining position of which it had long dreamed. Even though the Dixiecrats failed in their original purpose, they made the 1948 election close and therefore were an important factor in the campaign.

The Dixiecrat revolt was not a hastily conceived and irrational political aberration, but a well-organized and adequately financed movement designed to appeal not only to southern voters but also to all Americans anxious about governmental centralization in Washington. Thurmond and Wright were more than demagogic politicians; they were seasoned political leaders whose sincerity could not be doubted even though many voters rejected their ideas about states' rights, white supremacy, and concentrated political power. The Dixiecrats did not leave the Democratic party when they lost the election. They remained Democrats, hoping somehow to regain power within the party in the future. Long-tenured senators and congressmen retained their committee seats and chairmanships, but their support of efforts to play king maker blunted their effectiveness. Dixiecratic influence within the Democratic party began to disintegrate after the failure of the political apostasy.

The politics of the 1940s were politics of war and peace, preeminently, but by the end of the decade there could be no doubt that the black population of America, which was still concentrated in the South, had determined to take advantage of the national emergency to help create at home the sort of democratic conditions that the nation was seeking to advance abroad. In the work of moving black rights toward the center of the political stage, many forces and factors entered. The Roosevelt administration in its later years was as lukewarm toward black rights as earlier; the black experience lay remote from the president's life. But the civil rights issue was moving forward. When Truman came to the presidency he brought his own heritage of southern values, but he also brought an inquiring, active mind that could comprehend the problems of small people, not least blacks. Truman's political quandaries as his administration stumbled through its first months and years forced the civil rights issue toward the center of his administration's concerns. The reaction appeared in the Dixiecrat movement, a combination of purposes and prejudices that was less a movement than a demonstration. But Truman's victory in the election of 1948 made it clear that no retrograde efforts in the South would halt the progress of civil rights for black Americans, deflecting it from its course toward victory.

FIVE

The
Black
Revolution

Blacks began to make some headway during the 1930s in their drive for equality. While many New Deal programs and agencies were more helpful to economically depressed whites than similarly situated blacks, the fact that blacks were considered at all marked a revolutionary change in the ways of life in the South. Under the Works Progress Administration, American blacks for the first time in history received equal wages for the same amount of work as white men. A principle had been announced, even though it would take years to become established. The New Deal era heightened black consciousness and inspired rising expectations.

The Second World War then produced an atmopshere highly favorable to improving the status of blacks. Migration to the cities and to the North reached floodtide during the wartime emergency, as blacks took advantage of industrial expansion. The ideology of

the war also influenced black thinking. It was a war of democra-
cies against dicatorships; it was a fight in defense of freedom.
Blacks saw the contrast of war ideals with wartime practices and
determined to rectify injustice at home, to release themselves from
second-class citizenship. Black soldiers returning from the war
were outraged at the paradoxes in American life. If freedom for
other nations was worth dying for, then freedom for their own
race in their own nation was worth at least the sacrifice of their
lives.

If there was a third factor that helped prepare the way for the
black revolution of the 1950s and 1960s, it was the new situation
in national politics that followed Harry S. Truman's appearance
in the presidency. As set forth in the preceding chapter, Truman
by birth and upbringing was not the sort of individual from whom
one might have expected startling developments in regard to civil
rights. But this new president was a man with an open mind and
basically a man of extraordinary common sense. He found himself
pushed even beyond his own inclinations by the dissension within
the Democratic party, which drove him forward to advance the
rights of black Americans.

As the American South confronted its political and social
situation at the end of the war, and even during the years of the
Truman presidency, there must have been a considerable sense of
insecurity, a feeling that all was not right in the world, or at least
the world of the South as it had always existed. Southerners,
looking uneasily upon their heritage, had good reason for concern.
To their intense surprise, and only to a lesser extent the surprise of
all white Americans, a veritable black revolution broke out in the
early 1950s. This revolution was the predominant new fact of
American society in that decade, and it has dominated most social
and political changes in America down to the present. No other
internal sociopolitical change during the twentieth century has
affected, and probably will continue to affect, life in the United
States in so profound a manner.

THE EARLY YEARS

The revolution commenced with a struggle over an issue that
to an outsider might not have seemed germane to the major goals
of black Americans—the issue of school desegregation. In a drive
to desegregate the nation's public schools, the NAACP had
instituted several lawsuits that eventually reached the Supreme

Court. After a few years in the toils of the lower courts, there followed in May 1954 a most remarkable decision—*Brown* v. *Board of Education, Topeka,* in which the Supreme Court ruled unconstitutional the separate-but-equal concept in regard to public schools. Except for one or two outbursts in the nation's capital, the announcement of the 1954 decision did not provoke an immediate flood of protest from southern politicians. Since the Court waited a year before handing down an implementing decision, southern leaders were marking time. When the Court stated in 1955 that school desegregation must proceed "with all deliberate speed," southerners generally continued to remain silent, since the corollary decision did not set a specific timetable. If this wait-and-see attitude could have prevailed for a longer period of time, the South might have adjusted more easily to the inevitable. But social revolutions force politicians to choose sides, and most southern politicians followed their constituencies and southern traditions, as the southern populace awakened to the ramifications of the Court's decisions. Growing fears, rumors, prejudices, and publicity combined to awaken the southern population and its elected representatives. Senator Russell condemned the rulings as "a flagrant abuse of judicial power," and Senator Byrd denounced them as "this illegal demand" which he considered a serious blow to the "rights of the states." Senator Eastland, who believed that segregation was the way "of the Constitution, the laws of nature, and the law of God," announced that the South would refuse to obey the Court. He claimed that the Supreme Court justices had been "indoctrinated and brainwashed by leftwing pressure groups" and he did "not intend to permit a crowd of parasitic politicians who now sit on the Supreme Court bench to destroy those great institutions and the great culture which are in full flower in the Southern States—the culture of the Anglo-Saxon."

As opposition mounted, southerners in Congress announced a "Southern Manifesto" urging all members of the House and Senate "to join in the employment of every available legal and parliamentary weapon" to prevent school desegregation. Strom Thurmond, who originated the idea, prepared three early drafts. Byrd promptly endorsed the South Carolinian's plan, and the two senators circulated the proposal among southern delegations. Thurmond's bellicose wording was unacceptable to Senator Russell, and the Georgian signed only after he and an ad hoc committee rewrote the document. When several southern legislators still refused to sign unless additional truculent language was omitted, the document was twice more revised. The sixth and final draft was written by a committee of five senators: Thurmond, Russell, John Stennis of Mississippi, William Fulbright of Arkansas, and Price Daniel of Texas, the latter two being the spokesmen for those who preferred a more moderate document. This tempered version ultimately bore the signatures of 101 of the 128 national legislators from the eleven southern states: 82 congressmen and 19 senators. Forceful colleagues and constituencies exerted tremendous pressure to sign upon timid members of Congress, regardless of their own predispositions toward its principles; some signers apparently disagreed privately with the concepts advanced in the document. Senate Majority Leader Lyndon Johnson and House Speaker Rayburn were not invited to sign. Both Kentucky senators and the entire Kentucky House delegation were given an opportunity, but all refused, as did Tennessee Senators Albert Gore and Estes Kefauver. Kefauver announced his refusal to endorse the statement on the grounds that "the Supreme Court must be the final authority on constitutional questions. Its decision now is the law of the land and must be followed." Chaos and confusion could only result from flaunting a ruling of the Court.

In the minds of the manifesto's draftsmen, the Supreme Court had not followed the principles of the Constitution but had "substituted naked power for established law." They charged that the judges had exceeded their judicial powers and had "substituted their personal political and social ideas for the established law of the land." The manifesto reiterated that the principle of separate-but-equal facilities had become a part of the "southern way of life"; by rejecting it the Court had "planted hatred and suspicion where there had been heretofore friendship and understanding." The signers expressed support for the fundamental law of the land, criticized the Court's encroachment on states' rights, and encouraged the states to "resist forced integration by any lawful means." They suggested that southerners slow down judicial usurpation of power and use "all lawful means to bring a reversal of this decision which is contrary to the Constitution. . . ." Although they sanctioned the use of force against its implementation, they cautioned southerners not to be provoked into committing disorderly or lawless acts. The manifesto was not officially sanctioned by Congress; it was presented as a resolution, but its backers did not push it. It was primarily for public consumption in the South, and it probably confirmed the opinions of many that the Supreme Court had ignored the Constitution. It gave constituents hope that means would somehow be found either to circumvent or reverse the Court's ruling.

As southern opposition was crystallizing, the black civil rights movement was gaining momentum. A major catalytic agent was the Montgomery bus boycott of 1955–56. Heretofore, black-led boycotts had generally been unsuccessful, but blacks were determined to make this one a success. They formed the Montgomery Improvement Association and found a charismatic leader in a young Baptist preacher named Martin Luther King, Jr. With such organization and leadership they were able to force the city's transit company to operate desegregated vehicles. After the success of the Montgomery boycott, King and his followers organized the Southern Christian Leadership Conference (SCLC), which was soon coordinating nonviolent, direct-action activities throughout the South.

Black leaders across the nation were increasing their demands for national civil rights legislation. Northern politicians became more conscious of changing racial ratios and the consequent shift of political power in the great urban areas, and they introduced a spate of civil rights bills in Congress. Southern opposition fused immediately, and in July 1956 a second Southern Manifesto opposing passage of national civil rights legislation was issued. Drafted by Representatives William Tuck of Virginia, Colmer of Mississippi, and Edwin Willis of Louisiana, this "Warning of Grave Dangers" document was signed by eighty-three southerners. Like the first, the second manifesto both reflected and molded public opinion in the South. Since the days of Reconstruction, Congress had not passed a single civil rights bill for blacks. Although the filibuster was not the exclusive property of southern senators, over the years they had used it to their advantage to prevent civil rights legislation. In view of the events of the previous twenty years, however, the southern dam could not hold back the black rights movement much longer. The civil rights revolution was on the threshold of a historic breakthrough.

In 1957 Congress passed the first civil rights bill in the eight decades since Reconstruction. After the House had passed the bill, successful parliamentary maneuvers by supporters sent it directly to the Senate floor rather than to Eastland's Judiciary Committee, the deathbed of prior legislation. Extended filibustering techniques, including a record twenty-four-hour, eighteen-minute speech by Thurmond, only delayed the inevitable. The bill passed the Senate by a vote of seventy-two to eighteen. Southerners cast all the negative votes but one.

The Civil Rights Act of 1957 established a federal Civil Rights Commission with authority to investigate discriminatory conditions in the nation and to recommend corrective measures to the president. It provided for the establishment of a civil rights division within the Department of Justice; it empowered federal prosecutors to obtain court injunctions against those who interfered with the right to vote; and it allowed the Department of Justice to sue in cases where voting rights were being denied. It permitted the federal government to pay the expenses of all lawsuits of cases involving the violation of black voting rights, and it gave district courts jurisdiction over such lawsuits.

One must point out, unfortunately, that for all these advancements, the Civil Rights Act of 1957 proved less effective than its sponsors hoped. Individual lawsuits did not lead to widespread black voting, and few tangible results came from the Civil Rights Commission. Black leaders were disappointed in the ineffective measure; yet it was a significant psychological lift for their people. Blacks reasoned that if Congress could finally push through a civil rights act despite southern opposition, with additional pressures more effective laws might soon be passed.

But the black revolution was not to be put off. More pressures came in the spring of 1960 when four black students from North Carolina Agricultural and Technological College staged a sit-in at the lunch counter of a variety store in Greensboro. Because blacks had been required to stand when served at the counter in the past, the students sat on the stools at the counter and refused to move when ordered to do so. Before the spring had ended, hundreds of black students engaged in dozens of similar demonstrations throughout the upper South, the Atlantic coastal states, and Texas. Following the SCLC's nonviolent, direct-action approach and with moral and financial support from that organization, the college students' revolt was a decisive step in the civil rights revolution, as they successfully desegregated lunch counters in drug and variety stores. The campaign proved to be a failure in the Deep South, where arrests ran into the hundreds and where police brutality was evident in the breakup of the peaceful demonstrations. As tension increased and tempers flared, white southerners struck back, fighting the black students, setting fires in

A black protester in Memphis. (UPI)

black neighborhoods, and tossing bombs into recently desegregated schools.

There followed another congressional attempt at reform. After a tense summer, Congress passed the Civil Rights Act of 1960. The law made federal crimes of any flight to avoid prosecution for bombing offenses and willful interference to block federal court orders in regard to school desegregation. It also provided that in areas where the courts found a "pattern or practice" of discrimination, federal judges could appoint referees to hear persons claiming that state election officials had denied them the right to register and vote. Democratic Majority Leader Johnson had introduced the measure and with that action had become the first southern member of Congress since Reconstruction to sponsor a major civil rights bill of any kind. Except for Kefauver and Gore of Tennessee and Ralph Yarborough of Texas, Johnson's southern colleagues criticized his actions. Senator Thurmond said of the law: "This proposal is extreme. It is punitive. It is flagrantly abusive. It is palpably and viciously anti-Southern." Black leaders disagreed, condemning the act as too mild. In practice the law was hampered because, before its machinery could be started, the Justice Department had to present specific cases to prove that qualified citizens had been denied the vote on the basis of race or color. Blacks were encouraged, however, as they pondered the results of their direct-action strategy and the cumulative power of the passage of civil rights acts.

The civil rights drive continued when the Senate in March 1962 approved a constitutional amendment barring the payment of poll taxes for voting in federal elections and primaries. The battle to abolish poll taxes had nearly been won; only Texas, Arkansas, Mississippi, Alabama, and Virginia still required the taxes, but they did not constitute a major obstacle to black voting. The required number of state legislatures approved the Twenty-fourth Amendment in 1964, but since it applied to so few states and did not cover state and local elections, it was a symbolic gesture. Two years later the Supreme Court declared that state poll taxes violated the Fourteenth Amendment, and that device was at last laid to rest.

Southerners in Congress had fought the abolition of the poll tax, arguing that the states had the right under the Constitution to set voting requirements, but once the constitutional amendment had been accepted by Congress, they had no choice but helplessly to watch its progress through the required number of state legislatures. Some of them probably were frankly glad the long battle was over, even though it had been lost. For blacks, however, the battle had only begun. If southerners believed that the abolition of the poll tax would pacify black activists, they were mistaken.

SUCCESS

In the autumn of 1962 blacks began an all-out boycott of white merchants in Birmingham, in order to protest discrimination in restaurants, shops, and employment. Six months elapsed while the merchants remained adamant, even though business was suffering. In the spring of 1963 Martin Luther King, Jr., agreed that a massive demonstration was needed. Police Commissioner Eugene ("Bull") Connor refused to issue a permit for a march, but the blacks defied him. When scores of blacks were jailed as a result of the march, the Birmingham black community was aroused and mass demonstrations followed. City officials panicked and permitted fire hoses, electric cattle prods, and police dogs to be used to disperse the demonstrators. On the Monday after Easter, black children were encouraged to return to their churches to pray, sing, and dance. On the following Thursday, three thousand children skipped school to demonstrate in the streets. When they were jailed, too, more students demonstrated, and city officials could no longer cope with the size and momentum of the protests. Adults and older children staged additional sit-ins, which resulted in further confrontations with the police. Pictures of police dogs attacking black demonstrators damaged the South's and the nation's image around the world. The events in Birmingham spread to other southern cities; sit-ins, demonstrations, riots, and black-white confrontations occurred in Greensboro, North Carolina; Albany, Georgia; Selma, Alabama; Nashville, Tennessee; and many other cities. Some white southerners returned the blacks' anger point for point, but others were deeply troubled by these events. They believed that blacks should "remain in their place," but they could not condone police overkill or white retaliatory violence.

As these events aroused the nation, black groups and national leaders continued to press for legislative action. In February 1963 President John F. Kennedy delivered a special message on civil rights to Congress, stating that the time had come for the legislative branch to fulfill its obligations to black citizens as the executive had tried to do. Since less than 15 percent of voting-age blacks were registered to vote in five states (the Deep South states), Kennedy proposed that federal referees be authorized to register blacks while litigation was pending. To assist the black voter, Kennedy recommended that voting suits be dealt with ahead of other suits in the federal courts. He requested an act to standardize tests, criteria, procedures, or practices for all applicants who wished to register and vote in federal elections. He called upon Congress to pass his earlier proposal that a person with a sixth-grade education be considered literate as far as federal elections were concerned. To facilitate school desegregation, Kennedy suggested a program of federal technical assistance to aid school districts as they desegregated. Finally, the president asked that the life of the Civil Rights Commission be extended for four years and that it be empowered to act as a national clearinghouse to assist any private or public agency requesting its services. Bills were drawn up incorporating the president's requests, and hearings were held in the spring of 1963, but Congress failed to act.

In the meantime, the Civil Rights Commission had issued a highly publicized report calling the nation's attention to shocking conditions in Mississippi. The commission reported that blacks seeking to register to vote there had been "shot, set upon by police dogs, beaten, and otherwise terrorized." It noted that Leflore County had cut off federal surplus food allotments to seventeen thousand needy persons (mostly blacks) at the height of a registration drive. Whites and blacks alike across the nation condemned the complacency of Congress in view of such revelations. National frustration grew to anger in June 1963 when Medgar Evers, an NAACP official, was murdered in front of his home in Jackson, Mississippi. In a nationally televised speech a week later, President Kennedy referred to the racial crisis as a moral issue, and shortly thereafter he urged Congress to remain in session until it had enacted meaningful civil rights legislation. He preferred an omnibus bill with provisions for voting rights, equal accommodations, employment, federally assisted programs, education, and increased duties for the Civil Rights Commission. Kennedy realized that he would need public approval in order to get Congress to act favorably, and he and Vice-President Johnson spent hours in White House meetings attempting to secure widespread support.

In the summer of 1963 important black leaders organized and

led a march on Washington in order to dramatize the need for effective legislation to advance black rights. In August, while the president and vice-president were busy enlisting support for the omnibus civil rights bill, over two hundred fifty thousand people, nearly one-fourth of them white, converged on Washington to hear black leaders deliver addresses on the steps of the Lincoln Memorial. Martin Luther King, Jr., caught the imagination of the crowd as well as the nation with his "I Have a Dream" speech in which he articulated the recurrent dream that blacks might someday be fully equal citizens of American society.

President Kennedy had approved the march, but southern leaders in Washington were neither impressed nor inspired to act. Pressures continued to build, however, and in the following February an omnibus bill passed the House. Every section of the bill was an outrage to most southern senators, and as they had done in the past, they organized their forces to stop racial progress. The longest filibuster in Senate history occurred when the southerners talked for eighty-two working days; but in June the Civil Rights Act of 1964 was passed and signed into law by President Lyndon Johnson.

This was the most important law yet passed on behalf of minority groups. The major provisions of the act banned discrimination by businessses offering food, lodging, gasoline, or entertainment to the public; forbade discrimination by employers or labor unions when hiring, promoting, dismissing, or making job referrals; authorized government agencies to withhold federal money from any program permitting discrimination; authorized the attorney general to file suit to force desegregation of schools, playgrounds, parks, libraries, and swimming pools; tightened provisions to prevent denial of black voting rights in federal elections by declaring that any person with a sixth-grade education was presumed literate and that state literacy tests were not to be applied to him; established a federal agency to assist local communities in settling racial disputes; and granted additional powers to the federal Civil Rights Commission and extended its life until 1966. Alabama Governor George Wallace expressed the opinion of many white southerners toward the passage of the 1964 act when he declared, "This is a sad day for individual freedom and liberty."

In the middle of the summer of 1964 more violence occurred when white Mississippians resisted a voter registration drive by some two hundred volunteer college students from across the nation. Three of the students, one black and two white, were killed and buried in a shallow grave at a dam construction site near Philadelphia, Mississippi. Four other students were injured by gunfire, fifty-two were beaten, and over two hundred fifty were arrested for various reasons. Thirty black churches were damaged or destroyed during the summer, as whites used any methods to intimidate the blacks and their supporters. The voter registration drive in Mississippi was only one of many attempts to register blacks to vote in the southern states; some blacks had become convinced that the road to success passed through the voting booth.

The voting section of the Civil Rights Act of 1964 promised more than it could deliver, a weakness that stimulated King in January 1965 to lead a group of blacks in a registration drive in Selma, Alabama. When the drive did not succeed, King encouraged mass demonstrations in the streets and laid plans for a fifty-mile march from Selma to Montgomery, the state capital, to publicize the denial of basic political rights to Alabama blacks. Using tear gas and clubs, mounted police aborted the attempted march, but their violence spurred white citizens from other regions to rush to Selma to assist the black cause. Hoodlums savagely attacked four clergymen from the North; one of them, James J. Reeb, a white Unitarian minister from Boston, died two days after a brutal beating. A few days later King resumed his march to Montgomery, this time under the authority of a federal court order and protected by federal marshals, a nationalized Alabama militia, and dozens of FBI agents. Over twenty-five thousand marchers had gathered in Selma, although logistics permitted only a few hundred to make the four-day trek to the state capital. Governor George Wallace refused to meet King and his followers when they reached Montgomery, but King assured the nation that blacks would continue to press for their demands. Within hours of King's speech, Mrs. Viola Liuzzo, who had come from Detroit to support the march, was shot while driving demonstrators between Montgomery and Selma. The King-led march and the death of this white mother of five children were the immediate factors in causing Congress to pass an act to protect the rights of those who wanted to register and participate in the political process.

Then, at last, in 1965 came a major piece of federal legislation. The Voting Rights Act of 1965, passed after the Senate voted cloture for the second time ever in debate on a civil rights bill, provided for elaborate and effective federal machinery for registering voters and assuring the right to vote in areas where a literacy test was still required, and where less than 50 percent of the voting-age population voted or was registered to vote in November 1964. Federal examiners were given the power to decide whether blacks were qualified to vote in those states where voter discrimination had been most blatant. To be registered, an applicant merely had to fill out a simple form (with assistance from a registrar, if needed) giving his name, age, length of residence, and whether he had ever been convicted of a felony. If a person met these minimal qualifications, the registrar automatically added his name to a list of voters, and state and local election officials were required to accept the registrar's list. If they questioned the qualifications of a registrant, the challenge was to be heard before a federal judge and a decision made within two weeks. If an election was held during that period, the registrant was to be permitted to vote. Federal poll watchers were instructed to observe the actual election process, both the casting and counting of ballots. Anyone who intimidated voters or tampered with ballots faced stiff criminal charges and penalties. The need for this law was obvious. In 1965 in Sunflower County, Mississippi, the home of Senator Eastland, 80 percent of the county's 8,783 white residents of voting age were registered, but only 1.1 percent of the county's 13,524 blacks of voting age were on the rolls. This situation was so patently undemocratic that the United States Fifth Circuit Court of Appeals disallowed the 1965 election in the county. The Voting Rights Act of 1965 clearly closed many visible loopholes remaining from previous voting rights measures, and its supporters called it the most effective civil rights measure in the nation's history.

The worst racial violence occurred in the summer of 1967. Large sections of Detroit and Newark were burned down, and rioting, burning, and looting broke out from Seattle to Miami and from Los Angeles to Hartford. No major city was spared trouble, and even smaller towns experienced racial conflict as blacks across the nation continued to vent the frustrations of generations. In a special message in February of that year President Johnson had requested Congress to pass legislation designed to prohibit discrimination in the selection of federal and state juries, to enable the attorney general to initiate school desegregation suits, to forbid intimidation or physical harm of voters and civil rights workers, and to forbid discrimination in the sale or rental of housing by anyone selling or leasing more than three units in any

one year. Accepting the president's suggestions and in the wake of
the widespread rioting in the summer of 1967, the House of
Representatives passed a bill designed to make it a crime to harm
or intimidate persons exercising federally protected civil rights or
policemen and firemen trying to quell a riot or extinguish a fire,
and to make it a crime to cross state lines or use interstate
commerce facilities to incite violence. The bill was directed
toward both white and black activists. It died in the Senate
Judiciary Committee. Although no major civil rights bill was
enacted in 1967, the life of the Civil Rights Commission was
extended from 31 January 1968 to 31 January 1973, and a
clarifying provision was added to the section of the 1964 act
dealing with nondiscrimination in federally assisted school programs.

President Johnson signing the Civil Rights Act of 1968. (UPI)

Early in 1968 another comprehensive civil rights bill was
passed by both houses of Congress and signed into law by
President Johnson. Included in this new law were many of the
features of bills that had passed the House of Representatives
previously but had been stalled in the Senate. In addition, the
measure made it a criminal offense to manufacture, sell, or
demonstrate the use of firearms or other explosives to be used in

civil disorders, and it provided stiff federal penalties for persons convicted of intimidating or injuring civil rights workers. When President Johnson signed the act into law, he said: "We all know that the roots of injustice run deep, but violence cannot redress a solitary wrong or remedy a single unfairness. . . . And we just must put our shoulders together and put a stop to both. The time is here. Action must be now." It was significant that the bill was passed soon after the April assassination and funeral of Martin Luther King, Jr.

Black demands in their own behalf, which sometimes resulted in violence, and the responsiveness of national politicians to these demands and events were primarily responsible for passage of this series of civil rights acts from 1957 through 1968. Regional and national resistance by southern whites was not sufficient to halt a social revolution whose time had come.

SOCIAL AND ECONOMIC REVOLUTION

During the course of the black revolution in the 1950s, black demonstrators and northern politicians together forced profound changes upon the South's racial patterns. Jim Crow practices nearly a hundred years old were suddenly challenged and even swept away, and southerners had to face the fact that the Old South was gone. With this social revolution there was a simultaneous economic revolution; urbanization, the spread of commerce and industry, and changing racial relationships confronted southern politicians at the state level with problems whose number, complexity, and frequency they had never before imagined.

Southern segregationists were almost unanimous in their defense of white primaries and in their opposition to suggestions for a Fair Employment Practices Commission immediately after the Second World War, but for a while race remained a secondary issue in most of their campaigns, with the exception of the campaigns of Governor Herman Talmadge of Georgia. The Supreme Court decision in the *Brown* case in 1954 proved to be a turning point in southern state politics, dividing gubernatorial candidates into two groups. The first was composed of militant segregationists who deliberately catered to the racial fears of white southerners, berating the school decision and promising to resist federal authority over state schools. These militant governors reached peak numerical strength in the South in the late 1950s.

From 1954 to 1961 they won three-fifths of the governorship races, reflecting and encouraging the white South's repugnance to racial mixing. The 1957 school desegregation crisis in Little Rock, Governor Orval Faubus's personal response to the *Brown* decision, was a major factor in this militant upsurge. A mediocre governor at best, Faubus won a landslide reelection victory in 1958, just after he had defied federal authority and had received nationwide notoriety. At the same time, Virginia's program of "massive resistance," originated and named by Senator Byrd, became a systematic effort to thwart desegregation by legal devices. The state legislature repealed compulsory school attendance laws, withheld funds from school districts that permitted blacks to attend white schools, and provided tuition grants to parents of children who entered private schools when their public schools were closed. Byrd's handpicked governors such as A. S. Harrison and Lindsay Almond parroted the old master in racial matters, although Almond later disappointed Byrd when he softened his segregationist attitudes and presided over the downfall of massive resistance.

The second group of gubernatorial leaders were moderate segregationists. They generally shared the militants' objections to racial integration, but they preferred to play down the importance of the segregation issue. These moderates often promised to preserve segregation or limit desegregation, but they also expressed willingness to respect the decisions of the Supreme Court. Moderate candidates elected to governorships after 1954 included Carl Sanders (Georgia), LeRoy Collins (Florida), and Earl Long (Louisiana). In 1956 Long won an easy primary victory, due in part to heavy black support, and in the same year the moderate Collins won a clear majority in the first primary race over an opponent who ran an all-out segregation campaign. Collins hoped to preserve segregation, but he appealed to Floridians for "Christian tolerance" and observance of the law. In his 1957 inaugural address he told his audience that it should honestly recognize the realities of the South's position. Failure to do so would damage the moral welfare of Florida. He reminded them that the Supreme Court decisions were the law of the land. Carl Sanders's campaign in 1962 revealed the approach of a typical moderate segregationist. Sanders denounced his opponent, former governor Marvin Griffin, a militant on the race issue, as an "agitator." He promised to use "every legal means to preserve segregation, but he said he would never "put a padlock on a school door." He concluded: "I am a segregationist. I believe in equal opportunity but if I am elected governor I will not tolerate race-mixing." The political implications of moderation were not lost on the more ambitious governors. Frank Clement was governor of Tennessee when the school desegregation decision was announced in 1954, and he took the position that the public schools of Tennessee should continue to operate for the benefit of all of the children. Then in 1956 Clement and his advisers held a top-level conference to consider whether the governor should attempt to broaden his state following by favoring segregation or whether he should try to further his national image by maintaining his moderate position; Clement opted for the latter, but his stance did not advance his national political prospects.

Even though the public tried to force the school issue into the campaigns, the moderate segregationists preferred to remain noncommittal on the subject of race. They ignored the school issue and refused to declare that they would give token resistance to the Court decree, much less offer real resistance. Before 1960 no southern governors were yet willing to take pro–civil rights stands openly. The fact that a few successful gubernatorial candidates refused to be drawn into racial controversies was a sign of one of the most meaningful political changes in the modern South. In the next decade several governors would give active support to school integration, forever altering southern racial politics.

The major reason some governors soft-pedaled the racial issue was economic. They knew that racial disturbances brought undesirable publicity that could adversely affect the decisions of corporation executives who were considering locating industries in southern states. The moderate governors hesitated to defend segregated schools when they were trying to advance innovative, expensive, long-term economic development plans for their states. They often appealed to northern business leaders by pointing out the racial stability in their states, at the same time hoping that racial violence would not alter the picture.

The moderate governors were more aware of the relationship between economic advantage and the race issue than were their militant counterparts; but all southern governors recognized the increasing industrialization and urbanization in their region and campaigned for economic development. They adopted slogans such as "Balance Agriculture with Industry," bestowed tax exemptions and other favors upon manufacturers, and went on numerous industry-hunting tours of the Northeast and even

Europe. In his political autobiography, *Businessman in the State-house*, Governor Luther Hodges of North Carolina wrote that "industrialization . . . with all its advantages to the people and to the state, became the number one goal of my administration." Governor Faubus made creation and support of the Arkansas Industrial Development Commission a cornerstone of his administration's policy.

Although the goal of economic development was universally shared, the governors took different approaches to expedite economic growth. As time passed an increasing number of southern governors began to take the position that long-range economic development required greater state support for education, a necessary ingredient for the state's future industrial leaders and workers. They often campaigned on platforms calling for the creation or expansion of trade schools, community colleges, and state university systems. They seldom made direct references to education for blacks, although some educational funds were quietly used to upgrade black occupational training. As a result of the politicians' efforts more money was channeled into education, but the huge gap between southern and northern support of education was not noticeably narrowed.

Several successful gubernatorial candidates, such as A. S. Harrison of Virginia, Allan Shivers of Texas, and Jimmie Davis of Louisiana, minimized the financial responsibilities of the state. Harrison in 1961 attacked his opponent's "ultra-liberal approach to state finances" and he pledged to maintain Virginia's "sound, economical, constructive, progressive, honest government." The primary concern of Texas "Shivercrats" was fiscal responsibility, a long-standing southern tradition.

In a speech at Princeton University in 1960 Governor Collins of Florida expressed southern economic concerns well. He announced that the days of economic colonialism were ended and that the region was faced with "the challenge of accepting its part of the main stream of national life, and the responsibilities that go with it." He saw the region gaining in economic strength, but he believed it had to grow in moral strength and dedication to the nation's goals as well. He said: "If the South should wrap itself in a Confederate blanket and consume itself in racial furor, it would surely miss its greatest opportunity for channeling into a wonderful future the products of change now taking place. And the South must face up to the further fact that it would also bury itself for decades to come." He concluded, "Advocates of racial and

economic reaction—the very ones against whom we in the South
have to struggle on a local and state level for every inch of
progress we have made—[should no longer] be allowed to speak
for the South, simply because they have made the loudest noise."
Collins spoke for the majority of southern governors at the end of
the 1950s. Desire for economic development began to override
racial bias, and the decade of the 1960s appeared to be bright in
regard both to economic development and lessened racial tensions.

If one were to look for a single factor, once the black
revolution was under way, that forced more change upon the
South, it surely was the new access of black southerners to the
ballot box. This, certainly, had wrought a remarkable change in
southern politics and in southern society, too, as the blacks
worked upon the many inequities that had plagued their lives for
so long. Since the Second World War, and especially since the
1950s, court decisions and national legislation have combined to
permit more and more blacks to register, vote, and hold office. As
their numbers increase, blacks may ultimately have greater
influence than when whites were so preoccupied with their
disfranchisement.

The Supreme Court placed the first real wedge in the door of
the polling booth when it ruled in *Smith* v. *Allwright* (1944) that
the white primary was unconstitutional under almost any conceivable conditions. Subsequent decisions buried the subterfuge
totally. Before the historic 1944 decision, only about 250,000
southern blacks (5 percent of the black voting-age population)
were registered voters, and most of them cast votes only in
meaningless general elections or unimportant nonpartisan contests and referendums. Three years after *Smith* v. *Allwright*,
registered black voters had more than doubled in number and by
1952 the total had doubled again, to a level at which registered
blacks comprised about 20 percent of the potential (compared
with 60 percent of adult whites). The process continued, although
at a slower pace, so that by 1956 approximately 25 percent of
southern black adults were registered.

The civil rights acts of 1957, 1960, and 1964 all contained
provisions to help enfranchise black citizens. In 1960, 1,414,052
registered southern blacks constituted 28 percent of the total
potential, and between 1960 and 1964 the number increased by
about 500,000—the most rapid growth during any four-year
period since the end of the white primary. By 1964, 38 percent of

the southern black population was registered mainly because of
early civil rights efforts. The range was from a dismal 6.7 percent
in Mississippi to a respectable high of 69.6 percent in Tennessee.
Including Mississippi, a total of eight southern states had less than
50 percent of adult blacks registered. Florida and Texas joined
Tennessee with more than half of their qualified blacks on the
registration rolls. White southerners had found unofficial ways to
circumvent the intent of the laws on election day, however, and
southern states had used slowdown tactics ("legislate and liti-
gate") to blunt the edge of the voting rights provisions. Large
numbers of blacks were kept away from the ballot box by various
devices: limitations on the number of "registration days" each
month, broad discretionary powers in the hands of local registrars,
and literacy examinations. The travesty of democracy changed
dramatically with the passage of the Voting Rights Act of 1965,
and its renewal in 1970 assured continued progress. By 1970, 66.3
percent of voting-age blacks were registered. Even in Mississippi,
black registrations rose tenfold from 28,500 in 1964 to 285,000 in
1970, a truly astonishing increase. Statistics are more difficult to
obtain for actual black participation on voting days, but various
studies suggest that it has been considerable; approximately
two-thirds of the registered southern blacks voted in the 1972
elections.

In the wake of the Voting Rights Act of 1965 and the resultant
rise in registered black voters, black candidates often ran for and
sometimes won political offices in districts, counties, or towns with
sizable percentages of blacks. In 1965 only seventy-two blacks
held elective offices in the South, all at the local level. In the 1966
elections Lucius Amerson won the sheriff's race in Macon County,
Alabama, thus becoming the first black to hold a county elective
office in the South in the twentieth century. He was reelected to a
second four-year term in 1970. Also in 1966, sixteen blacks won
local offices in five heavily populated black counties in Mississippi, and ten others won places in runoff primaries, only to be
defeated by slim majorities. Generally blacks ran for local jobs
such as city councilman, tax collector, district constable, justice of
the peace, district and county supervisor, member of boards of
education, and deputy sheriff. Events in Greene County, Alabama, showed what could happen in regions where blacks were
numerous and politically active. In 1962 Greene County had only
174 black voters, but by 1968 that number had risen to 3,988.
With a four-to-one population majority and a two-to-one voting

majority, in a special election in 1969 that county's blacks gained
political control by electing four of their race to the five-member
county commission and winning two of the five places on the
county school board in addition to the one they had occupied
since 1966. In the general election of 1970 six more blacks were
victorious: a sheriff, probate judge, coroner, circuit clerk, and two
more members of the school board. "It isn't the end of the world,"
said one defeated white official, "it just seems like it." Another
distraught white candidate acknowledged that the 1970 vote
"pretty much polarized the feeling in the county, but I think the
white people are getting over it. They'll learn to live with it. Some
have moved away, but most of them will stay." Standing beside
his deputies—two black, one white—Sheriff Thomas Earl Gilmore
took the oath of office in January 1971 and then commented that
Greene County "is the beginning of a new hope for America."
Whites still control what economic power there is in this
admittedly poor rural county, but the black officials have shown
that they are as capable of running the county government as their
white predecessors. As blacks gain more experience and as the
whites who remain recover from the trauma of lost political
power, Greene County may very well develop responsive and
effective government, and this will be all for the good of the
county's previously neglected black citizens.

Blacks were elected to state legislative bodies. Leading this
political parade was Julian Bond, publicity director for the
Student Nonviolent Coordinating Committee and son of Horace
Mann Bond, the well-known historian and dean of Atlanta
University. Winning 82 percent of the vote in one of Atlanta's
largely black districts, Bond was elected to the Georgia House of
Representatives in June 1965. The state legislators seated seven
other blacks at the beginning of the session in January 1966, the
first to serve in the assembly since 1907, but they denied Bond a
seat, allegedly because of his opposition to United States involvement in Vietnam but in reality because he had been a leader in
black organizations involved in sit-ins and demonstrations. While
one thousand demonstrators marched on the state capitol in
Atlanta to protest this action, Bond filed suit in federal district
court to obtain his seat. In a two-to-one decision the court upheld
the principle of legislators passing upon the qualifications of their
new colleagues and therefore refusing to admit Bond. While
Bond's appeal was pending before the Supreme Court, he was
again elected to the Georgia legislature, and again the legislature

refused to seat him. The Supreme Court ruled that Bond's rights were being denied and in January 1967 Bond was seated without protest. Other districts also elected blacks to state assemblies, so that by 1970 every southern state legislature had at least one black member and several had a half dozen or more; by 1972 there were sixty-one in the eleven states.

In 1969 Charles Evers, brother of Medgar Evers, was elected mayor of Fayette, Mississippi, a town whose population of sixteen hundred was 75 percent black. Inspired by Evers's success, other blacks ran for and won mayoralty positions. After the 1972 elections thirty-eight blacks served as southern mayors. With a population of five hundred thousand evenly split between whites and blacks, Atlanta elevated vice-mayor Maynard Jackson to its top position in November 1973, making the Georgia metropolis the first large city in the South to be led by a black. At the same time C. E. Lightner was elected the first black mayor of Raleigh, North Carolina, a victory more significant for the future than Jackson's, since Raleigh's population of one hundred twenty-five thousand was 75 percent white. Lightner was one of nearly a dozen black mayors who presided over majority-white constituencies. If blacks regularly begin to win leadership posts in the South's medium-size, majority-white cities, a significant political milestone will have been reached.

Democrat Charles Evers ran for governor of Mississippi as an independent in 1971, knowing that he had no chance to win the Democratic primary. In a field of seven in the Democratic primary, Evers openly supported radio country singer Jimmy Swan, who stumped the state brandishing a copy of Theodore Bilbo's book, *Take Your Choice: Segregation or Mongrelization*. Evers had calculated that the racist Swan would be the easiest Democrat to beat in November, but Swan ran a poor third in the first primary. Eventually Evers faced William Waller, a moderate Jackson attorney best known for having twice unsuccessfully prosecuted a segregationist for the 1963 murder of Evers's brother. Waller overwhelmed Evers 544,000 to 158,000. Evers was probably mainly responsible for his own overwhelming defeat. Ten days before the election, he threatened to file suit to disqualify his opponent for having exceeded state spending limits in the Democratic primary. Coupled with an intense black voter registration drive, this feint panicked Mississippi whites into a huge voter drive of their own. They realized that if Waller were disqualified, Evers would automatically win the election. Evers did not carry

through on his threat but Mississippians quaked at the prospect of
a black becoming governor under any circumstances, and they
woke up to the fact that they could no longer afford to be
politically apathetic. Waller's large victory followed an unprecedented 70 percent turnout of registered white voters for the
election. Registered blacks were outnumbered two to one, and less
than two-thirds of them voted.

In the same election, the total number of black elected officials
rose from ninety to one hundred. Sixteen blacks ran for sheriff and
nine ran for chancery clerk, but all lost even though the contests
were in areas with black majorities. Blacks did elect one tax
assessor, three additional county supervisors, and a few justices of
the peace. Robert Clark, the only black member of the legislature,
squeaked through by three hundred votes, despite a newly
gerrymandered district. But these were isolated triumphs, hardly
infringing upon the established white power structure and certainly not helpful to Evers if he had national political aspirations.
Evers's hopes for an assault on the governor's mansion by a
black-led coalition were shattered for the time being, but Mississippi blacks would never again be politically invisible. Numbers of
elected black officials in Mississippi had risen from zero in 1965 to
145 in 1973—more than in any other state. But the trend was
South-wide; after the 1972 elections, 1,144 blacks held elective
state and local offices in the South accounting for about half of all
elected blacks in office throughout the nation.

So a succession of changes had thrust themselves upon the
South, within two decades after the end of the Second World War.
The New Deal, the war itself, and the Truman administration had
prepared the way. Then the issue of school desegregation had
raised black hopes as never before. The novelties of the 1950s and
the 1960s were extraordinary, unprecedented, remarkable—the
words of observation tended to prove insufficient when any
student of the South, conversant with the ways of that region for
all the years of its history, observed what had happened within a
short generation. To be sure, everything had not been solved in
the relations between the races; there were many areas where
further change was highly desirable, even mandatory. Consider
the fact that black officeholders seldom proved successful beyond
election to minor, local offices. It was difficult to get many blacks
to register and then to vote; like their white brothers, they tended
to stay at home on crucial occasions. There were still large areas
of the American South where agriculture was the principal

economic reliance; and in such places, where illiteracy was not uncommon, the business of getting out the vote was extraordinarily difficult. But whatever the troubles or problems, there were increasing numbers of trouble solvers ready to face them—blacks and whites alike, but increasingly there were blacks. The black revolution had seen to that. The new awareness of the promise of American life had changed the lives, literally, of millions of black Americans. Not least, it had revolutionized the lives of southerners.

Presidential Republicanism in the South

If a twentieth-century southerner during the years before
1945 had been heard to say that a state of his section, or several
states from his section, might go Republican in presidential
elections, any individual hearing such a judgment would have said
that so opinionated a person was out of his mind. Not that
southerners in times past had refused to vote the Republican
ticket. Although Democrats had dominated the region's politics
after the Compromise of 1877, Republican presidential candidates
had continued to receive sizable percentages of southerners' votes.
In the presidential election of 1880—during which the Solid South
is usually said to have emerged—more than 40 percent of all
voting southerners cast their ballots for the Republican nominee.
In eight of the eleven former Confederate states, the Republican
ticket garnered a larger proportional vote in 1884 than it did in
1880. Even though all southern states cast their electoral ballots

for the Democratic candidates in these and in the presidential elections of 1888, 1892, and 1896, Republican voting strength remained strong in the South to the end of the nineteenth century. Before 1900 Republican presidential nominees sometimes captured as much as 49 percent of the total votes in some southern states, and often no less than a third. If Republicanism declined after the turn of the century, a small but persistent vote for Republican presidential candidates continued. Herbert Hoover in 1928 won the votes of five southern states. Even so, modern presidential Republicanism received its greatest boost from the Dixiecrat revolt of 1948. Even though the Dixiecrats considered themselves "true" Democrats and desired to remain in the national Democratic party, their actions caused thousands of grassroots Democrats to vote for—or seriously consider voting for—a presidential candidate who was not a Democrat. After their first non-Democratic vote, it was easier to pull other than Democratic levers thereafter. Presidential Republicanism in the South increased markedly in the 1950s, 1960s, and early 1970s.

"THE SOUTH LIKES IKE"

Senators Estes Kefauver and Richard Russell actively campaigned for the Democratic nomination in the spring of 1952. Thus, two southerners—one liberal, one conservative—aspired to the highest office in the land. Kefauver was too liberal for his native South; he had supported the amendment to liberalize the Senate's cloture rule, had endorsed voluntary compliance with FEPC rulings, and had favored federal antilynching legislation if the states did not act. In contrast, Russell opposed anti–poll tax bills, antilynching legislation, and the FEPC. The Georgian announced that if he received the nomination he would refuse to endorse any civil rights plank in the party's platform that was favorable to FEPC. Kefauver said he would be morally bound to support the platform even with a powerful FEPC included. In Florida's primary in May, Russell won nineteen and Kefauver five of that state's twenty-four votes in the national convention. These results increased the Democratic party's problems. Russell was unacceptable to northern liberal Democrats, and Kefauver had no friends among the big-city bosses because the Tennessean had linked organized crime with Democratic urban machines when he presided over hearings into crime in the nation in 1951.

President Truman encouraged the Democrats to consider

Illinois Governor Adlai E. Stevenson for the nomination. Because
Stevenson believed that states were responsible for abolishing
discrimination in employment (although he favored federal laws if
the states did not act), South Carolina's Governor Byrnes
endorsed him. Thus, Stevenson had the support both of the
retiring president, who continued to stress that civil rights progress
should be an issue in the campaign, and of Byrnes, who had
opposed Truman since 1948. Stevenson himself was cool toward
the nomination and publicly stated that he preferred to remain
governor of Illinois. On the eve of the national convention, the
Democrats were still casting about for a nominee who would be
acceptable to both North and South; a compromise seemed
inevitable.

In the meantime, Republicans were showing interest in
General Dwight Eisenhower as their nominee. Eisenhower, a
career military officer, had never taken public stands on domestic
issues until the preconvention campaigns got under way. At that
time he remarked—rather ambiguously, as was his style—that he
was "somewhat" opposed to federal FEPC legislation. He also
stated that he had "tried to eliminate segregation in the armed
services [where] we can no longer afford to hold on to the
anachronistic principles of race segregation. . . ." This contra-
dicted a statement he had made in 1948 in which he said he was
not prepared to go beyond the integration of black platoons into
white companies. At the Republican convention, civil rights was
not a major issue, but it was not entirely ignored. The convention
adopted a civil rights plank that was considerably weaker than the
one the Republicans had approved in 1948, an indication that the
GOP was shifting its accent from federal action to a renewed
emphasis on state initiative, a stand more acceptable to the South.
But the platform was incidental to the candidate; the popular
Eisenhower swept the nomination, and his prospects for winning
the presidency appeared excellent.

In contrast to the Republicans, the Democrats faced a
potentially divisive battle over their platform. Northern liberals
hoped to retain or extend the 1948 civil rights plank, while
southerners, who wanted to leave civil rights in state hands,
preferred not to mention the issue at all. The platform committee,
whose fifty-two members included both Senator John Sparkman
of Alabama, and black Congressman William Dawson of Chicago, hammered out a compromise. The 1952 plank was similar to
the one adopted in 1948, but as a *New York Times* editorial said, it

'THERE'S SOMETHING ON THAT LINE!'

Roy Justus, *Minneapolis Star*, 1952

lacked "the fighting words that would have immediately caused another full-scale Southern bolt." Southerners were not enthusiastic about the Democratic platform, but they did not walk out of the convention, partly because the convention had earlier pointedly refused to bind all delegates to support the party's nominee in advance.

The Democrats nominated Governor Stevenson to head their ticket, indicating a wish for unity. Stevenson's moderate racial views were acceptable to the South, and his stand on labor, business, and welfare attracted northern liberals. The choice of Senator Sparkman as Stevenson's running mate further served to reveal the drive for harmony between North and South. However, Sparkman's nomination offended blacks, since the Alabamian had voted with the southern conservatives on civil rights. The Democrats reasoned that Stevenson would attract northern liberal and black votes and that Sparkman would hold the South in line. Polls showed that most black voters intended to vote for the Democratic ticket despite the presence of Sparkman. The blacks' attachment to the Democratic party was primarily economic, and the civil rights stand of Sparkman was a secondary consideration. When a black laborer was asked how he felt about a southerner running for vice-president, he replied, "That don't mean anything. I'm a working man. How can I vote anything but Democratic?" The Democrats appeared to have a winning combination, but as Stevenson cultivated northern black votes he lost ground in the South where the civil rights issue was the white voter's principal concern. When Louisiana's Governor Robert Kennon proclaimed that he would not support the ticket and when James Byrnes reversed himself and announced that he would vote for General Eisenhower, Republican chances of winning some southern states increased. Eisenhower welcomed this support as well as that of Senator Byrd and Governor Shivers of Texas, and he campaigned in the South stressing his opposition to FEPC and standing and clapping when bands played "Dixie."

Eisenhower won the election by a vote of 442 to 89 in the electoral college. Northern blacks had remained loyal to the Democratic party, but Eisenhower's popularity with white voters had negated that bloc as populous northern and western states such as California, Michigan, New Jersey, New York, Ohio, Pennsylvania, and Wisconsin went Republican. The Eisenhower appeal spilled over into the South, too, as Virginia, Tennessee, Florida, and Texas cast their electoral ballots for the Republican ticket. Although black voters were not numerous in Louisiana and South Carolina, in this close election their votes for the Democratic ticket were all that kept the general from carrying these two states. Eisenhower carried only 35 percent of the popular vote in Alabama, as that traditionally Democratic state remained loyal. Not without significance were the results of the voting in Mountain Brook, the most economically and socially exclusive white suburb of Birmingham, where 2,996 voters supported Eisenhower and 755 voted for Stevenson; by contrast, at a polling place in the inner city of Birmingham where all qualified voters were black, the votes for Stevenson and Eisenhower were 256 and 64, respectively. Similarly, upper-income white precincts in Charlotte, North Carolina, cast about 85 percent of their votes for Eisenhower, while all-black precincts in that city ranged from 80 to 90 percent for Stevenson. The patterns in Birmingham and Charlotte were common in other southern cities: wards and precincts that went overwhelmingly for Eisenhower invariably coincided with upper-income residential areas, and districts heavily inhabited by black voters without exception went for Stevenson by large majorities.

Eisenhower's great personal attraction was primarily responsible for his landslide victory, but in the South his vote totals reflected the alienation of southern Democrats from their own party. "Democrats for Eisenhower" clubs were formed, barbed reminders to regular Democrats that Dixiecrats remained disaffected though reluctant to join the Republican ranks permanently. The same sentiment was expressed on auto bumper stickers throughout the South: "I'm a Democrat but I like Ike." The Dixiecrat separatist movement of 1948 was not repeated in 1952, but its former supporters were clearly drawn to Eisenhower, his moderate but nebulous stand on civil rights undoubtedly being a significant factor. This was the first time the so-called Solid South had been broken since 1928, although the Dixiecrats had muddied the waters in 1948.

Middle-class white southerners' affinity for Eisenhower and black voters' support for Stevenson had important ramifications for future southern politics. Many observers saw Eisenhower's appeal in the South as a significant boost for the weak Republican party there, but the more perceptive also noticed that Democrats had won state and local elections. Eisenhower won a victory for presidential, not grass roots, Republicanism. The challenge for southern Republicanism was to make presidential election successes help local party candidates. The Democrats faced a challenge of a different order: could the party continue successfully to appeal to both white supremacists and black voters? The long-range questions of whether the South in 1952 was on its way to becoming a genuine two-party region and whether the Democratic party could reconcile its factions had not yet been answered.

Soon after the Supreme Court handed down the historic school desegregation decision in May 1954, President Eisenhower instructed the District of Columbia commissioners to take the lead in desegregating their schools as an example to the entire country. Washington's schools opened in the autumn of 1954 under a policy of nonsegregation. Eisenhower did not believe that integration was the only way to achieve equality; he warned in private that "social disintegration" might result if the beliefs of white southerners were not respected in the matter. Social equality did not mean that "a Negro should court my daughter." He said, "You cannot change people's hearts merely by law." In his memoirs, the president reminded his readers that at the time he refused to say whether he either approved or disapproved of the school decision. Since the Court's judgment was law, he said that he would abide by it. After his retirement, he said that he "definitely agreed with the unanimous decision," but the nation found little positive guidance from the White House in the early stages of a momentous social revolution. The South was pleased with the president's lack of vigor in enforcing the school desegregation decision.

Throughout most of his first term, Eisenhower consistently refrained from pushing for civil rights legislation. Then in the spring of 1956 his administration introduced a proposal calling for a new bipartisan civil rights commission and a civil rights division under a new assistant attorney general, new laws to aid in enforcing voting rights, and amendments to existing laws that would permit the federal government to seek in civil courts preventive relief in civil rights cases. The House of Representatives passed a bill to establish a civil rights commission and a civil rights section in the Justice Department, but it died in Eastland's Senate Judiciary Committee. Democrats accused Eisenhower of introducing the measure to get northern black votes in the forthcoming election, knowing well that southern senators would not permit such a bill to pass and would thus be blamed for lack of progress on the civil rights front rather than the Republicans.

'A CLOUD NO BIGGER THAN A MAN'S HAND'

Roy Justus, *Minneapolis Star*, 1956

'GREENER PASTURES?'

Somerville in *The Atlanta Journal.* 1957

Adlai Stevenson, who had been reluctant to run in 1952, was less hesitant in 1956 and accepted the pressure from many prominent party members to run again. Senator Kefauver was his vice-presidential running mate. Despite its balance, the Democratic ticket had little chance of winning against the popular incumbent. Stevenson ran "with all the zest and decisiveness of a man taking the final steps to the gas chamber," according to one political observer. Eisenhower's electoral victory of 457 to 73 was coupled with a margin of more than nine million popular votes.

Stevenson and Kefauver carried only seven states, six of which were southern Democratic strongholds: North Carolina, South Carolina, Georgia, Alabama, Mississippi, and Arkansas. Since Eisenhower captured the remaining five southern states and many individual votes in all the southern states, political observers again suspected that the so-called Solid South had been broken. A close look, however, revealed that southerners were still splitting their ballots. Like many northern Democrats, southerners continued to support Democratic candidates for congressional seats in state and local elections while voting for the popular Eisenhower for the presidency. They were receptive to Eisenhower's middle-of-the-road policies at a time when more and more of them felt alienated from the national Democratic party and the people and policies dominating it. Republican registrations did not increase in the South during the Eisenhower years, but southerners were becoming more flexible when casting their ballots.

The Independent States' Rights movement added another factor to the election of 1956. Several southern Democrats were disgruntled with the Supreme Court's school desegregation decision of 1954 and with the increasing trend toward national civil rights legislation. Led by South Carolina's Governor George Bell Timmerman, these politicians worked to organize a third party. They held conventions and conferences in the summer of 1956, but it soon became clear that they had only a small numerical following and lacked the endorsement of major political leaders. But these few intransigent conservative southerners and scattered northern sympathizers still hoped for a neo-Dixiecrat party. They endorsed T. Coleman Andrews and Thomas H. Werdel for president and vice-president. Andrews was a Virginian and former director of Internal Revenue; Werdel, a former Republican congressman from California. Despite the enthusiasm of its supporters, the Independent States' Rights movement failed to develop into a viable political alternative. The Andrews-Werdel

ticket appeared on the ballots of only five southern states and
Wisconsin, and nominal campaigns were undertaken in Louisiana, Tennessee, and Virginia. The Independents gained some
popular support only in Mississippi and South Carolina, but
states' rights leaders in those two states rejected Andrews and
Werdel, formed a splinter group, and eventually endorsed Senator
Byrd for president and Representative Williams of Mississippi for
vice-president. The Byrd-Williams ticket won 29 percent of the
vote in South Carolina and 17 percent in Mississippi, siphoning
off much of the white protest vote that had gone to Eisenhower
four years earlier in black-belt counties and in silk-stocking wards
of Charleston and Jackson. The Independents carried less than 10
percent of the votes in the remaining southern states. Most
dissident southern Democrats preferred to remain in their party,
continuing to support Democratic candidates for state and local
office but choosing to revolt against the national organization by
voting Republican in the presidential election. Dissidents saw no
real advantage in voting Independent, and they were satisfied with
the still popular Eisenhower, his political philosophy, and his
stand on racial issues. Having voted for the Republican candidate
in two successive presidential campaigns and having voted
Dixiecratic previously, many southern Democrats were making a
habit of not voting for their party's nominee. Presidential Republicans appeared to be gaining a toehold in the South.

KENNEDY AND JOHNSON

Sending about one-quarter of the total delegates to the
national Democratic conventions every four years, the South had
always advanced a presidential candidate, not with the expecta-
tion of winning, but at least with the hope of influencing the
platform. Lyndon Johnson of Texas represented the South in
1960—but as a serious contender rather than a token favorite son.
He had an almost endless supply of political experience, having
served in the national legislature continuously since 1937. He was
a practical politician, a shrewd bargainer, and a legislator who saw
more value in compromising on an issue in order to win a partial
victory than in clinging idealistically to a principle on the way
down to total defeat. During the Eisenhower years, as Senate
majority leader, he had cooperated with the Republican president
better than many members of the president's own party. These
qualities gave him leverage within his own party as well as

national recognition and potential national appeal. Sitting firmly on a solid power base, the South's Johnson bypassed the primary contests, knowing that he carried with him to the national convention the kind of political support that would make him a leading contender for the nomination.

As the winner of numerous state presidential primaries, Senator John Kennedy of Massachusetts was the Democratic front-runner. Protestant prejudice toward a Catholic aspirant still existed, a handicap Kennedy had to work hard to overcome. When he won, by a decisive margin, the primary in West Virginia, a border state where Protestants constituted 95 percent of the churchgoing population, Kennedy established himself as an effective vote getter in Protestant country, and the odds of his receiving the nomination were increased appreciably.

Johnson—who had repeatedly stated that Kennedy was too young and inexperienced and that the nation really needed a man "with a touch of gray in his hair"—appeared to be the only serious obstacle in the path of the Kennedy juggernaut. But Kennedy and his well-oiled and well-heeled organization, led by a band of youthful but able politicians, had done their work thoroughly and Kennedy won the nomination on the first ballot. Kennedy then tapped Johnson as his vice-presidential choice. Knowing that the religious issue would cut into his voting strength, particularly in the South, Kennedy reasoned that with the Texan as his running mate, Protestant southerners and midwesterners might be less inclined to stray from Democratic ranks. Johnson had become a spokesman for limited black civil rights in recent years, but Kennedy wagered that southerners would continue to accept Johnson as one of their own. Johnson's association with old-line Democrats, many of whom were powerful southerners, would be of great benefit to the Democratic ticket in the November balloting.

The South's Protestant fundamentalism and anti-Catholicism made Kennedy's religion extremely critical in this campaign. He was aware that no Catholic had ever been elected president and that Democrat Alfred Smith's Catholic religion had been an important factor in his defeat in 1928, when five southern states had strayed from the Democratic fold and thousands of voters in the remaining six states voted for the Protestant Herbert Hoover. Recognizing the importance of clearing up southern reservations about his religion, Kennedy accepted an invitation to discuss his religious beliefs before the Greater Houston Ministerial Association in September. In a carefully prepared statement he declared that church and state should remain separate, that no Catholic prelate should tell a Catholic president how to act, that no church or church school should be granted public funds or political preference, that no man should be denied public office merely because his religion differed from the president who might appoint him, and that the religion of the president of the United States was his private affair. Kennedy then answered impromptu questions reflecting areas of Protestant concern over Catholic policy. When he had finished, he had defined the personal doctrine of a modern Catholic in a democratic society more fully and explicitly than any other thinker of his faith. The news media and Kennedy's faithful followers highlighted the statement and his forthright answers to the pointed questions at Houston, and thousands of voters who had been attracted to Kennedy but who had previously held doubts about a Catholic in the White House were mollified. Without question, the Houston experience played a large role in subduing the Protestant South's fears about a Catholic president. The issue was effectively dismissed: Richard Nixon avoided discussing religion in his campaign against Kennedy, and Kennedy made no overt religious appeals in areas of heavy Catholic concentration, to the credit of both.

Both Nixon and Kennedy openly courted the nation's growing black vote. Kennedy's coup was a sympathetic telephone call to Mrs. Martin Luther King, Jr., when her husband was jailed after leading a civil rights demonstration in Atlanta. Several southern governors had advised Kennedy against commenting on King's civil disturbances on the grounds that he would harm the Democratic cause in the South, but Kennedy ignored the warnings. The phone call was widely publicized, and it undoubtedly brought about the Democrats' narrow victories in several states.

The Democrats won a razor-thin victory in November. Kennedy received 303 electoral votes to Nixon's 219. Mississippi was carried by a slate of eight independent electors who, along with six electors from Alabama and one from Oklahoma, voted for Senator Byrd. But the electoral votes did not tell the whole story. Kennedy out-polled Nixon by only 119,450 votes out of a total of 68,836,385. Nixon carried the normally Democratic border states of Oklahoma and Kentucky as well as the southern states of Tennessee, Virginia, and Florida. He polled 46 percent of the total vote cast in the eleven southern states and chalked up great numbers and percentages in the suburbs of the South's

Sandeson in The Ft. Wayne News-Sentinel

"His hollowed ground!"

Sandeson in *The Fort Wayne News-Sentinel*, 1960

industrial centers: Dallas, Houston, Birmingham, and Atlanta. Signs of a stronger southern Republicanism were unmistakable. Under the circumstances, Kennedy's selection of Johnson at the convention a few months before turned out to be crucial; the southerner's presence on the ticket may have been the difference between victory and defeat for the Democrats. According to NAACP estimates, Kennedy received nearly 85 percent of the total black vote across the nation, and Nixon later claimed that he could have won the election had he campaigned harder for the black vote. In the electoral college Kennedy would not have carried Illinois and Michigan without the black vote; had these states gone Republican Nixon would have won. Interestingly, Texas, North Carolina, and South Carolina were held in the Democratic column by black votes. Thus, southerner voters— both black and white—were vital to the outcome of the election.

Whatever his intentions in regard to the advancement of black civil rights, President Kennedy had to face reality as soon as he became president: if he pressed too hard for civil rights legislation, he would alienate southerners whose votes he needed on other important matters. To avoid betraying blacks, however, he decided to use his executive powers to further civil rights rather than to work through Congress. For two years he and his attorney general (his brother, Robert Kennedy) relied primarily on executive orders and litigation for civil rights progress. In the summer of 1963, when the nation was experiencing considerable racial tension, unrest, and conflict, Kennedy finally called upon Congress for effective legislation.

Presidential adviser Theodore Sorensen has written that John Kennedy gave little thought to blacks except in terms of their votes until he became president of the United States. Harry Golden wrote, "I do not think that either the . . . President or the Attorney General was fully aware of the enormity of those wrongs [against blacks] when they took their oaths of office." This lack of prior commitment and the president's willingness to delay and compromise on civil rights legislation may indicate that he was a political opportunist. More important is the fact that Kennedy finally did commit himself to advancing the black cause, and he built solidly upon the base laid down by prior presidents. A final assessment of his administration in regard to civil rights is impossible; but Kennedy certainly did not endear himself to southerners on the issue, and had he lived he would undoubtedly have encountered even more resistance from the South than during his first years in office. His untimely death probably forestalled a direct confrontation and a showdown.

Lyndon Johnson was shocked as were two hundred million other Americans when John Kennedy was shot in Dallas, Texas, in November 1963. He quickly stepped into the vacancy, however, and as if to emphasize the importance of continuity, one week after taking the oath of office he briefly addressed Congress at which time he listed several "immediate tasks," the first of which was the passage of Kennedy's civil rights bill. The Civil Rights Act of 1964 was passed in the following June. Other civil rights laws were also passed, and Johnson continued executive action in the tradition of Presidents Truman and Kennedy. Johnson's five years in the presidency saw more legislation passed in the field of civil rights than any other five-year period in American history. In view of the fact that Johnson was a southerner, no more ironic action could have been taken by Congress—with the full support of the president.

Although Johnson's efforts in behalf of black Americans made him a "traitor" to his native region in the eyes of some southerners, in other ways he satisfied the southern electorate. A tax reduction measure was so pleasing to the South that Senator Russell, longtime leader of the southern bloc in Congress, announced his support of Johnson for president and essentially precluded a Dixiecrat-type revolt in 1964. In truth—despite the civil rights issue—southerners in Washington and at home were among President Johnson's most loyal supporters.

In 1964 the Republicans chose as their candidate Senator Barry Goldwater of Arizona, an outspoken political conservative. Goldwater urged the curtailment of federal programs in the interest of greater freedom for the individual and the states and crusaded against an all-dominating, all-entangling federal bureaucracy. Although claiming that he personally opposed racial discrimination, he indicated that he would leave the protection of civil rights to the states. Many white southerners were attracted to the Arizonan because of his support of states' rights and the more than obvious implication that he was unsympathetic to rising demands for black equality. (In June he had voted against the civil rights proposal.) Riots in many of the nation's largest cities in the early summer of 1964 had contributed to the passage of that civil rights act, but they also created a white "backlash" that the results of the 1964 campaign dramatized.

Goldwater carried his home state of Arizona, plus Louisiana,

Mississippi (where he won by an astounding 87 percent), Alabama, Georgia, and South Carolina. Alabama exemplified what
was happening to the southern states in presidential elections. In
1952 Alabama had cast all eleven of its electoral votes for the
Democratic nominee; in 1956 one elector had voted for an
Independent nonentity; in 1960 six of eleven electors had voted
for the Independent candidacy of Senator Byrd; and in 1964 the
state switched to the Republican nominee. In only twelve years,
Alabama had moved from solidly Democratic to solidly Republican in the presidential elections. Although blacks who voted in the
five Deep South states supported President Johnson's reelection,
Goldwater's popularity with white voters won him those states'
electoral votes. Goldwater would also have carried Arkansas,
Florida, Tennessee, and Virginia if blacks had not voted so
overwhelmingly for Johnson. In the eleven southern states,
Goldwater drew 49 percent of the total vote; the GOP was
obviously willing to appeal to southerners on the basis of implied
racism.

The early months of the 1964 presidential campaign had been
confused by the candidacy of Alabama's George Wallace. Like
the Dixiecrats of 1948, Governor Wallace had become disenchanted with the national Democratic party's recent civil rights
policies, and he hoped to throw the 1964 election into the House
of Representatives, where he would have considerable bargaining
power. Unlike the Dixiecrats, however, Wallace did not restrict his
campaign to the South, and he entered several Democratic
primaries in northern states. Most observers saw Wallace's
campaign as a joke until he polled 34 percent of the votes in the
Wisconsin Democratic primary. A few weeks later he received 30
percent of the votes in the Indiana Democratic primary and 42.7
percent of the primary votes in Maryland. As Wallace suspected,
his segregationist platform appealed to voters outside the South,
forcing regular Democrats to take his candidacy seriously. Stating
that he had accomplished his mission to "conservatize" the
candidates of both major parties and that he did not need to
continue as a candidate, Wallace withdrew from the race before
the national conventions. Since he and Goldwater had somewhat
similar political beliefs, Wallace realized that his continued
candidacy would only assure the "liberal" Johnson's reelection.
But even without Wallace in the field, Johnson swamped Goldwater in a race that saw southern blacks voting for a southern

white, while about half of the southern whites voted against the first resident southern president since Andrew Johnson.

The controversy over the nation's increasing involvement in the Vietnam war soon marred Johnson's popularity; at one time he complained that he was not being given "a fair shake as president because I am a Southerner." Southerners as well as northerners were criticizing Johnson, however, and in the face of increasing criticism and dwindling support he chose not to run for a second full term in 1968. His presidency had stalled the southern trend toward presidential Republicanism, but only temporarily. The Republican era that followed LBJ's political demise not only renewed the trend but also began to solidify Republican strength in the South on all levels of political reality.

THE NIXON STRATEGY

Richard Nixon's successful bid for the presidency in 1968 constituted a significant chapter in the history of presidential Republicanism in the South. In the spring of that year, Nixon won several northern primaries, but he felt he needed more support in the southern states to be assured of the Republican nomination and the election. Accordingly, Nixon met in Atlanta with important Republican leaders in the South, including Texas's Senator John Tower and South Carolina's Thurmond, who after flirting with the Republican party for several years had jumped the political fence in 1964. Southerners hoped for more than a cursory role at the forthcoming convention and they wanted reassurances about the philosophy of a possible Nixon administration. On civil rights—the major concern of the southern Republicans—Nixon stated at Atlanta that the Supreme Court's phrase "all deliberate speed" needed reinterpretation, and he suggested that new Supreme Court justices should be conservative in philosophy. He opposed compulsory busing of school children from one district to another to achieve racial balance, and although he insisted that federal funds should not be given to school districts practicing segregation, he did not favor withholding federal funds from a school district while it and the federal government took months to agree upon an acceptable school desegregation plan. Nixon assured southerners that they would participate in decisions both at the convention and in a future Nixon administration. Southerners wanted their share of federal patronage, and Nixon guaranteed they would get it. After the Atlanta meeting, Nixon was assured of southern support at the Republican convention, and he easily won the nomination. Tower and Thurmond pressed Nixon to pick a conservative for his vice-presidential running mate, their favorite being California's Governor Ronald Reagan, but they did not object when Nixon settled on Maryland's Governor Spiro Agnew, a border state moderate.

Nixon and the Democratic nominee, Hubert Humphrey, had to contend with George Wallace, who was again a presidential candidate. Wallace entered Alabama politics when he was elected to the state legislature in 1946. Six years later he became a circuit judge and in 1958 he ran for governor for the first time. When he lost the contest to a right-wing racist, Wallace announced: "John Paterson out-niggahed me. And boys, I'm not goin' to be out-niggahed again." Keeping his promise, he was elected governor in 1962 on a racist platform. In his inaugural address he pugnaciously shouted: "I draw the line in the dust and toss the gauntlet before the feet of tyranny. And I say, Segregation now! Segregation tomorrow! Segregation forever!" Wallace became a national figure when he ran for the presidency in 1964 and brought out the not so latent racism of nonsoutherners. When he withdrew from the presidential contest that year, he announced that his foray into national politics was not over, and by 1967 he was gearing up for the next race. To an interviewer in early 1968, Wallace summarized what he thought the issues would be in the coming presidential election: federal interference in local schools, including busing for racial balance; law and order versus crime in the streets; the liberal Supreme Court; federal restrictions over the sale of private homes; heavy federal taxation; and the war in Vietnam, which he believed the United States should make an all-out military effort to win. Four of these six issues were directly or indirectly related to the nation's racial problems.

Wallace organized and ran a clever campaign as the candidate of the American Independent party. He was able to place his name on the November presidential ballot in every state in the Union. Early polls showed that Wallace consistently appealed to only about 10 percent of the voters, and his candidacy was generally ignored. But then his poll totals began to rise, and they took a large jump after the Democratic convention, which had coincided with violence in the streets of Chicago. The nation was forced to take the Wallace candidacy more seriously, and some

observers predicted that he might capture as much as 30 percent
of the total votes in November. More importantly, Wallace could
prevent either Nixon or Humphrey from winning a clear majority
in the electoral college. Wallace hoped to take seventeen southern
and border states for a total of 117 electoral votes, enough for the
standoff in the general election. But that was not enough; he
scouted for votes in northern urban centers, and both Humphrey
and Nixon realized that he could affect the balance in key states in
the North. But the more Wallace campaigned, the farther behind
he got. While he appealed to an alienated 10 percent of the
population, his campaign of hate and distrust did not catch on
with the majority. His prized epithets—"pointyheaded intellectuals," "government pussy-footing," and "sissy britches welfare
people"—began to wear thin as the campaign heated up. Many
who earlier had been inclined to be sympathetic to Wallace turned
against the "wildman."

The Wallace movement faltered at the very time the Humphrey organization began to make headway. By the day of the
election Humphrey had pulled even with Nixon in the polls. When
all the votes were counted the breakdown showed that Nixon had
won a plurality of only 510,315 of over 73 million cast. Nixon won
301 electoral votes; Humphrey won 191; and Wallace took 46, all
from Alabama, Arkansas, Georgia, Louisiana, and Mississippi,
plus a lone vote from North Carolina.

Although Vietnam was a major issue that year, the differences
between candidates on the subject were not clear-cut, and the
principal controversy in the campaign was over race—"law and
order" in Wallace's vocabulary—which explains the strength of
the Wallace vote. He won half his popular vote total outside the
South, chiefly among white workingmen. In no less than thirty
states he managed to affect the balance of power; Humphrey or
Nixon won clear majorities in only twenty states. Wallace's
percentage of the vote total was not sectional; however, his totals
showed how many southerners were willing to put race over party.
Wallace won nearly 5 million votes in the former Confederate
states. The Democrats won only 31 percent of the total votes in
the South, and southern blacks probably cast two-thirds of those.
Nixon won the electoral votes of Florida, South Carolina,
Tennessee, and Virginia, plus all but one in North Carolina. Only
Texas among the southern states remained in the Democratic
column, probably because many Texans reasoned that a vote
against the national ticket would have represented a repudiation

of native son Johnson. If Wallace had not run, Nixon might have
carried ten of the eleven southern states. Some people professed
they could visualize a solid Republican South in the near future,
and the Republicans surely had an opportunity to strengthen their
party in that conservative region.

Before the 1968 election, Nixon made the deliberate choice of
trying to appeal to southern whites rather than to the nation's
black voters. His long-range political plans called for the ardent
wooing of white southerners in order to develop Republican
voting strength in the former Democratic stronghold. This strategy—which the Nixon administration never acknowledged—
subtly catered to the segregationist impulses of white southern
voters while it claimed only fair treatment of the South.

In a meeting in April 1970 between Nixon and thirty-five of
the highest-ranking black officials in the federal government,
Health, Education, and Welfare assistant secretary James Farmer
informed the president that there was "a growing spirit of [black]
hopelessness that the Administration is not on their side" resulting
from a public posture taken by Nixon that seemed overtly
antiblack and anti-integrationist. The president's public position
in turn stemmed from his desire to combine the 1968 Nixon and
Wallace voters in the South for a Republican majority in 1972. He
realized his debt to the South for both his nomination and
election; the payment of that debt became the guiding rule for his
civil rights policies and his dealings with the black minority during
his presidency.

In carefully phrased campaign speeches and presidential
statements, Nixon implied that he would move to slow down or
even reverse the process of school desegregation in the South. By
choosing his words deliberately he received approval from southerners without alienating less racist supporters outside the South.
The Nixon strategy of "go slow" was quite apparent in the
summer of 1969. Federal courts had directed several Mississippi
school boards to draw up plans for complete school desegregation,
and by August schemes worked out in conjunction with HEW
advisers were ready to be presented to the Fifth Circuit Court of
Appeals for approval. Then in a reversal initiated by the president,
HEW Secretary Robert Finch asked the judges of the court to
grant a delay in the submission of desegregation plans until at
least 1 December to avoid "chaos, confusion, and a catastrophic
educational setback. . . ." The federal government urged such a
delay in court, and the court granted the request. In a landmark

ruling on 29 October, the Supreme Court reversed the circuit court decision. In a curt, blunt statement the Court announced its unanimous decision that segregation in thirty-three Mississippi school districts—and by implication throughout the entire South —must cease "at once." The justices declared that procrastination of school desegregation amounted to nothing less than "the denial of fundamental rights to many thousands of children." The president said he disagreed with the Court's decision, but since it was the law of the land, his administration would enforce it. Nixon had placed himself in an enviable position vis-à-vis the South: he ingratiated himself with the region even as he was required to carry out the Court's order.

The most explosive issue at this time relating to southern politics and schools was the question of busing children for the explicit purpose of achieving school integration. White southerners were against busing for this purpose, and southern politicians took up the cry. Nixon had aligned himself with white voters in the South and had given white southerners hope that the school movement could be slowed down, that some form of token integration might satisfy the laws and the courts. Segregationists were convinced that they had a friend in the White House for the first time in many years. Nixon's concern for the South at times was too much for one of his political managers who said on one occasion: "The South . . . the South, I'm so goddamn tired of hearing about the South. When is somebody going to start worrying about the North? That's where the votes are, to begin with. Instead we're fighting over the law in order to give something to a bunch of racists."

Nixon's conservative philosophy, his unhappiness with the Supreme Court (including its recent "at once" decision), and his promise to southern Republican leaders that he would encourage the Court to move in other directions led the president to seek to fill a vacancy on the Court with a southerner. When Abe Fortas left the Court in May 1969, the president was not impressed with the fact that the seat had been filled for fifty-three years by Jewish justices and nominated Clement Haynsworth, a quiet and proper judge from Greenville, South Carolina, who sat on the Fourth Circuit Court of Appeals. Labor lawyers and civil rights advocates discovered that Haynsworth had been unsympathetic to labor and that he had a conservative record on civil rights. Further investigation revealed that the judge had served on the board of directors of companies involved in cases in his court and that he had purchased stock in a company while he was deciding the fate of a suit against the company. It made no difference that Haynsworth made no money because of these decisions or that his broker had purchased the stock for him without his knowledge; the suggestion of carelessness was enough for the Senate to reject (forty-five to fifty-five) the nomination in November 1969. All southern senators except Gore of Tennessee and Yarborough of Texas voted for the South Carolinian's appointment. Seventeen Republicans voted against it. The president was most unhappy with these defectors and with the outcome of the vote. In anger he made it clear that he still intended to name a justice with these qualifications: white, southern, a strict constructionist with experience on the federal bench, under age sixty. One White House aide said privately to another, "You know, the president *really* believes in that Southern strategy—more than he believes in anything else."

As if to underscore that belief, Nixon nominated G. Harrold Carswell, a judge on the Fifth Circuit Court of Appeals, a native of Georgia then living in Tallahassee, Florida, who had run for the Georgia legislature twenty-two years earlier on a segregationist platform. Most senators discounted Carswell's early statements, but they were concerned about the judge's current attitudes on the subject of race—investigations showed that Carswell was a member of a segregated Florida country club and that his land covenant barred blacks from buying homes in his neighborhood. Although Carswell insisted he believed in equality of the races, the Senate was not swayed, particularly when "mediocrity" seemed to be the epitome of Carswell's years on the bench. The Senate rejected the nominee by a vote of forty-five to fifty-one, Gore and Yarborough being joined by Fulbright and William Spong of Virginia in the vote total against Carswell. Had these four southerners reversed their votes Carswell would have been confirmed. In an obvious pitch for southern identification and votes, Nixon said, "I understand the bitter feeling of millions of Americans who live in the South at the act of regional discrimination that took place in the Senate yesterday." Fulbright responded: "I think regional aspects were of no importance. I could suggest some southerners I am quite sure would pass with little opposition." Many southerners knew that Fulbright and others could list a dozen possible choices better than Nixon's nominee, and they were frustrated and disappointed that Nixon had not presented the best the region had to offer. The vacant seat was at last filled when the Senate approved without difficulty the nomination of Minnesotan Harry Blackmun.

After eighty-five-year-old Supreme Court Justice Hugo Black retired in September 1971, President Nixon at last was able to name a southerner to the Court, when the Senate accepted the nomination of Lewis F. Powell, Jr., a Virginia lawyer. Powell was impeccable in every respect, even though he was known to be a civil rights conservative. He was the first southern conservative to be confirmed since 1941, when Byrnes of South Carolina had been approved. Powell's overwhelming acceptance discounted earlier remarks that the Senate would not confirm any southerner, and many wondered why the Nixon administration had waited so long to tap a really qualified person for the Court.

The president's style, his rhetoric, and his tone were important factors in Nixon's popularity in the South. He used the code words southerners wanted to hear, and the symbolism of his actions was unmistakable. Clearly he was on the side of the South, the white majority, and the status quo. Nixon had increased southern Republican strength for the 1972 campaign, but the costs were high: increased racial division, disillusionment of civil rights leaders, and serious problems between the administration and members of Congress.

The primary goal of the "southern strategy" was to convince white southern Democrats that they should support President Nixon despite their party affiliations. The replacement of southern liberal Democratic senators and congressmen with moderate or conservative Republicans who would support the president and his programs and the building of state and local Republican parties in the South were only of secondary importance. Although Nixon unfailingly kept his eye on the 1972 presidential campaign, being sure that he took no actions to jeopardize his personal support in the South, in 1970 he attempted to implement the secondary goals of the "southern strategy." When it became evident that these aims were not necessarily compatible with winning the presidency again, Nixon made clear what was more important to him. While he verbally supported building his party at the state level, he was mainly concerned about presidential Republicanism.

NIXON VERSUS WALLACE

That Richard Nixon would be a candidate for reelection in 1972 was never in doubt. Much of the president's energy had been spent during his four years in office in preparation for a second term, and Nixon and Agnew were renominated in an atmosphere of supreme confidence that they could be reelected. In contrast to the tightly controlled Republican primaries and convention, the Democratic contest was wide open. Among the sixteen serious candidates was, again, George Wallace. When he announced for the Democratic nomination, he said that he was a national, not a regional, candidate and that he believed he best represented the people's attitudes on the major issues of the day. Furthermore, he said he fully expected to win the nomination, but that if by chance he did not, he would then decide whether to run as an independent in the general election. As he said, "I'm gonna shake up the Democratic party. I'm gonna shake their eyeteeth out."

During the long primary season eleven of the candidates ran in the Florida contest, including Wallace. The ballot also listed propositions concerning school busing, equal education, and prayer in schools—issues made to order for Wallace's emotional appeals, which he exploited with the canny skill of a political winner. All over the state, Wallace ran through his litany of campaign themes: opposition to school busing, calls for law and order, and a strong national defense, appealing to racial bias on two of his three major points. The other candidates knew that Wallace was the man to beat in Florida, and they accordingly directed most of their fire toward him. Wallace, aware that a sizable majority of all Floridians considered busing the most important single issue (about 65 percent, according to one poll), was buoyant as he told his audiences: "All six of them [past and present senators in the race] voted or announced in favor of busing to achieve integration. I advocate . . . a tranquil and stable school system on a non-discriminatory [but separate] basis." Referring to his opponents' stands on busing—some of which had shifted as they felt Florida's pulse—Wallace said, "There is more pluperfect hypocrisy in this election than ever before." When it became clear that Wallace would win the Florida primary, the other candidates jockeyed for the prestige of second place in a large field. The results of the election showed Wallace winning with a whopping 42 percent of the total vote, larger than the combined votes of his three closest challengers.

Wallace not only loosened some Democratic eyeteeth; he also stimulated the Republicans into action. Two days after Wallace's primary victory, Nixon delivered a fifteen-minute, nationally televised address in which he committed the full power and prestige of the White House to the war on busing. The president had long opposed busing for racial balance, but the scope of the new program that he was sending to Congress made it clear that he was determined to make the busing issue his own. He promised that his plan would "end segregation in a way that does not result in more busing," an objective that had perennially eluded courts, legislatures, and education officials. The president proposed a moratorium until July 1973 on new court-ordered busing, strict new limits on how the courts could deal with continued school segregation, and the channeling of $2.5 billion of federal funds to impoverished schools. Nixon's most vociferous critics charged that this combination was a retreat to the discredited "separate but equal" educational doctrine. The president gave reason for these fears: "What I am proposing is that at the same time we stop more busing we move forward to guarantee that the children currently attending the poorest schools in our cities and rural areas be provided with education equal to that of good schools in their communities." For all the administration's disclaimers, civil rights leaders saw the president attempting to turn back the tide of school desegregation. From a short-range view, of course, the president's proposal was good politics. Even if the antibusing steps were ultimately found unconstitutional, the pace of busing would be stalled during the long legal wrangle that would last until after the November election.

Wallace's candidacy made Nixon realize that southerners who were disenchanted with the national Democratic party's liberal stand on civil rights would not necessarily vote Republican. Wallace had latched on to an issue that would keep or bring back straying southern Democrats into the party's fold, if he could get the nomination. Dissident southerners had more allegiance to the issue of race than to the Republican party or its presidential candidates. Wallace's candidacy reminded Nixon of that, and Nixon set out to undercut Wallace on the busing issue—the most emotional issue of the campaign and the one with which southerners were most concerned.

After Florida, Wallace focused on Wisconsin, Pennsylvania, Indiana, Tennessee, North Carolina, Michigan, and Maryland, states where he had run well in 1968 and which he believed would again be responsive. He was determined to project a national image in the South and Midwest. To the surprise of many, Wallace finished second in the primaries of Wisconsin, Pennsylvania, and Indiana, and first in those of Tennessee and North

Carolina. So warm was Wallace's reception in the northern states
(42 percent of the votes in Indiana, for example) that he seemed
more than ever resolved to press his cause within the Democratic
party and to lay aside any third-party defection plans.

Michigan was aflame over a controversial court ruling on the
busing issue. Nowhere outside the South had antibusing demonstrations been more fierce than in the suburbs of Detroit. Large
crowds responded enthusiastically to Wallace as he talked straight
to those in sympathy with his views. Maryland's primary was to be
on the same day as Michigan's—16 May—and Wallace spent
some time campaigning in that friendly state too. But the day
before the primaries while Wallace was campaigning in Maryland,
he was shot by a young man with a small handgun in full view of a
crowd of spectators and television cameras. Wallace was para-
lyzed from the waist down and hospitalized for an indefinite
period. Fear of his imminent death was premature, but statements
from his wife and his staff that they would carry on the campaign
were not taken seriously. If his political career had not ended,
Wallace's presidential hopes appeared to have been temporarily if
not permanently smashed. Assassinations and attempted assassinations have constituted a long-standing blot upon the American
democratic process; in Wallace's case the event was particularly
tragic. Dual primary victories in Michigan (51 percent of the vote
in a three-man race) and Maryland (39 percent of the vote in a
three-man race) combined with earlier victories showed that
Wallace had considerable strength in both North and South and
that he was gaining momentum.

In a wheelchair, Wallace spoke to the Democratic national
convention; although he was awarded polite applause, his presence and speech had no impact upon the proceedings. The
convention chose South Dakota's Senator George McGovern as
its candidate. Southern delegates were unhappy with the convention proceedings, the liberal platform, and their candidate.
Realizing that his political philosophy was generally unacceptable
in the South and preferring to focus on the large electoral vote
states, McGovern virtually ignored the South in 1972. His liberal
image, his stand for minorities, his statements on busing (he
favored limited busing to correct racial imbalance), and his
opposition to the Vietnam war alienated many southern conservatives. Few Democratic politicians in the South actively campaigned for McGovern, and those running for office often urged
voters to split their tickets. In the past local candidates had been

happy to cling to the coattails of the national candidate; in 1972 most candidates ignored McGovern and some openly disavowed any association with his candidacy or his philosophy. In Georgia Democratic senatorial candidate Sam Nunn frankly told voters that he would vote for Nixon, and Nixon-Nunn billboards were common. The leader of the drive in Virginia to reelect Nixon said McGovern's philosophy was "alien to the majority of Virginians." Organized labor in the South supported the Democratic candidate, but except in Texas it did not have enough strength to influence an election.

Since Texas was one of the eight largest electoral states, since Nixon had failed to carry the state in 1960, and since Texas was the only southern state which had voted Democratic in 1968, the Democratic candidate did give that state some attention. McGovern himself made four trips there, one of which included an address to the Texas legislature. He visited former President Johnson and received his endorsement, but Johnson made no other statements and campaigned not at all for the South Dakotan. Eleanor McGovern made a trip into Texas for her husband's cause, as did other national Democratic figures, including vice-presidential candidate Sargent Shriver, but the force of conservatism in Texas guarded the national ticket from overoptimism.

John Connally hampered McGovern's campaign in Texas—and in the remainder of the nation, for that matter. The former Democratic governor of Texas, administrative assistant to Lyndon Johnson, and secretary of the navy under John F. Kennedy had joined the Nixon team as secretary of the treasury in December 1970. Rapidly mastering the myriad intricacies of economic policy, Connally became one of the president's closest advisers. After eighteen months and while at the height of his influence in Washington, Connally resigned to return to private life, and shortly thereafter he spearheaded the "Democrats for Nixon" movement. Connally made it clear that he was a registered Democrat, and he even announced that he would support Texas Democratic candidates. He appealed to those Democrats in the South and across the nation who opposed McGovern and who were willing to vote for Nixon without any thought of changing party affiliations. Connally's organization proved helpful to the president—financially as well—but many southern Republicans were unhappy. They had worked for years to build the Republican party in their states, and they wanted to encourage the crossover

registration trend that would help not only the president but also
the struggling state Republican parties throughout the South.
Except for Florida and Texas, Connally wisely kept his lieutenants
out of the South, although he personally visited George Wallace in
his Birmingham hospital room to plead unsuccessfully for a Nixon
endorsement.

Nixon made a one-day trip to Atlanta for a downtown parade,
and later in the campaign he made a forty-minute stop at a North
Carolina airport in behalf of a Republican senatorial candidate.
He was so confident of winning in the South, however, that he
made few campaign appearances there; for the most part he sent
his surrogates. Vice-President Agnew visited several southern
states, including Virginia, Tennessee, Florida, and Texas. Secretary of the Treasury George Shultz and New York congressman
Jack Kemp campaigned for the president in the Lone Star State.
In an effort to win the Spanish-speaking vote, Nixon dispatched to
Texas Mrs. Romana Banuelos, treasurer of the United States.
Nixon made an overnight swing through Texas in mid-September,
but this was his only personal effort.

Southern Republicans were unhappy with the president's
neglect of their region during the campaign. Nixon made few
statements in support of southern Republican senatorial and
congressional candidates, fearful of touching off resentments that
might cost him Democratic votes for his own candidacy. Texas
television stations ran a political advertisement showing the
president and Senator Tower together, but Tower's supporters
openly critized Nixon for not giving more help in what appeared
to be a close contest. The president's aloofness also caused
bitterness in other states. Nixon's former postmaster general,
Winton ("Red") Blount, who appeared to have a chance to
become Alabama's first Republican senator since Reconstruction,
asked for a personal appearance from the president; he got Tricia
Nixon Cox instead. Nixon's desire for an overwhelming personal
mandate did little to move the South in the direction of a
two-party system. Nixon himself scrupulously avoided Deep
South states where powerful Democratic chairmen in Congress
were heavily favored for reelection, refusing to support their
Republican opponents for fear of offending politicians who would
surely return to Congress. Since he needed legislative support
from these conservative Democrats, this was good politics for the
president, but it did nothing to build the Republican party in the
South. The administration openly supported one Democrat.

Attorney General Richard Kleindienst paid a two-day visit to Mississippi and the home of James Eastland, who as chairman of the Senate Judiciary Committee had worked hard for President Nixon's Supreme Court nominees. Kleindienst said that if he were a Mississippian, he would vote for Eastland. Southern Republicans were concerned with strengthening their party however, and they resented Nixon's personal political game.

President Nixon won 61 percent of the vote to McGovern's 38 percent, and John Schmitz, a John Bircher from California who headed George Wallace's old American Independent party but who did not receive Wallace's endorsement, won just over 1 million votes for 1 percent of the total. A large portion of Nixon's votes came from Wallace supporters. Wallace had won more popular votes than any of his competitors in the various Democratic primaries before he was shot in Maryland, and these Democratic voters overwhelmingly (nearly 85 percent) turned to Nixon rather than McGovern in November. If Wallace had been in the race, he would surely have won most of the southern states, and he may have taken enough votes away from Nixon in some northern states to give McGovern their electoral totals. In all likelihood Nixon would have won the election anyway, but the distribution of the electoral totals conceivably could have been far different. But without Wallace Nixon's electoral totals constituted more of a landslide than did his popular majority. The president won 49 states for an electoral total of 521, while McGovern won only Massachusetts and the District of Columbia for 17. The landslide proportions of the campaign put it in the same category as Johnson's win over Goldwater in 1964 (when Goldwater won five states) and Roosevelt's win over Alfred Landon in 1936 (when Landon won two states). Since Nixon had retained a low profile throughout the campaign—he actually made overtly political visits to only fourteen states—he did not help Republicans running for Congress, and both the House and the Senate remained Democratic. This resulted in one commentator referring to "President Nixon's lonely landslide"; this election was certainly not a victory for the Republican party as a whole.

As had been true in the two previous presidential elections, southerners cast more votes on a percentage basis for the Republican nominee than did the rest of the nation. While Nixon's nationwide percentage was 61, his percentage in the South was 71, ranging from 66 in Texas to 80 in Mississippi. With so many Democrats pulling Republican presidential levers, the election of 1972 was unprecedented in American history as the Republican candidate carried every southern state. By that year voting Republican in presidential campaigns had become a habit for many southerners.

It was an interesting, even fascinating, situation—the South voting Republican on the presidential level. What it might mean for the region's future was of course almost impossible to say. But then, in an area of the country which for years had seen very little dissension over national politics—the South had fought its issues in the Democratic primaries, or else not fought them at all—the appearance of a choice in presidential elections meant essentially a new sort of enfranchisement for southerners. Dissent in presidential elections was bound to work its way back into regional politics on the state and county levels, and some of this working would undoubtedly occur because of national support for this or that southern issue, in hope of gaining some possible further benefit on the national level; it perhaps would be inadvertent support for change on the state and local levels, but support nonetheless.

This increasingly presidential Republicanism of the South had affected the region's politics, quite apart from federal legislation over civil rights issues, quite apart from agitation of black southerners for their own civil rights. Will the South as a whole, facing the new possibility of voting Republican or Democratic in presidential, state, and local elections, still choose the course of conservatism? Will conservatives continue to shift back and forth, from party to party, to maintain their principles through the threat of further shifts? Will the Republican party in the South remain content to dominate in presidential elections only, or will it work diligently to convert conservative southerners to their organization as well as to their candidates? Solid Democracy has certainly been shaken up; but with the stirrings of Republicanism a new "democracy"—a new openness in the southern political process—has begun to take hold.

SEVEN

The
New Politics
of the South

As late as 1952, Alexander Heard in his perceptive book *A Two-Party South?* could write that "to many citizens of the South, a Republican is a curiosity. They may have heard about the Negro undertaker who goes to Republican conventions . . . but a genuine, breathing Republican is a rarity in most of the counties of the region." But then came a great change. The southern wing of the Republican party transformed itself into an organization almost completely different from what it had been before, and the twentieth century at last caught up with the South.

The reasons for the change were many. Growth of industry throughout the region gave more southerners a feeling for the traditional philosophy of the Republican party. Industrial development attracted many northern Republicans to the South as executives and managers, and in innumerable instances they helped provide new leadership for the party. As cities rapidly increased in size, many southerners moved into suburban houses and purchased two automobiles, swimming pools, and all the other symbols of affluence; for them, too, the Republican party's values reflected their own desires and fears. Longtime conservative Democrats, who earlier had had no alternative when the national Democratic party displeased them, migrated to the Republican party. Still another factor in the South's new politics deserves mention: namely, that the new southern Republicans were serious about their political allegiance; they were no fair-weather party members. Some possessed the zeal of converts, and others were simply infected by their party's new energies. Whatever the reasons, they wanted to be serious opponents of the Democrats, nationally, on the state level, and locally. Republicans began to run candidates for the House of Representatives with hopes of winning. By the early 1960s they were winning; in 1962, Republican House candidates contested 62 seats and polled 2,083,971 votes. By 1964, all but 138 of the 1,140 counties in the eleven southern states possessed active Republican organizations.

THE DECLINE OF ONE-PARTYISM

Serious Virginia Republicanism dates from 1949, when moderate-to-liberal Democrat Francis Pickens Miller entered the Democratic primary for governor against the Byrd machine's candidate, State Senator John S. Battle. When it appeared that Miller had an even chance of defeating Battle, conservative Democrats urged Republican voters to cross over and vote for Battle in the Democratic primary. He won, but by less than a majority (42 percent of the vote), and Republicans realized that their votes might have made the difference. This result stimulated them to organize for future contests. In 1952 Miller took on Byrd himself in the Democratic primary for U.S. senator. Byrd won easily, however, gaining potential Miller votes as he directed his wrath at Harry Truman and Truman's presidential candidate (Adlai Stevenson), just falling short of endorsing the Republican presidential aspirant. Byrd's conservative followers helped Eisenhower carry the state, the first time Virginia had gone Republican since 1928. Although their senatorial candidate had lost, Virginia Republicans were encouraged by the state's evident Republican leanings, and in 1953 their gubernatorial candidate, Ted Dalton, won 45 percent of the vote after an intense campaign directed at the conservative Democrats of the Byrd machine. The Supreme Court decision of 1954 compelled the state's political leaders to address the issue of school desegregation, and the massive resistance fight caused deep divisions within the Byrd organization's ranks, moderate Democrats showing considerable disappointment in Byrd's stand against desegregation. The Democratic state convention's endorsement of President Johnson for reelection, a decision that went directly against the known views of Byrd and the organization's governor, was symptomatic of the weakening of the machine; such a direct challenge was unknown in previous Byrd-era Virginia politics. Byrd's pledge of total resistance to integration also hardened Republican opposition. Meanwhile, Republicans increasingly had been winning campaigns for local offices, and this contributed to the mood of dissatisfaction within the dominant organization.

Virginia Republicans ran moderate Linwood Holton for the governorship in 1965 with more than a little hope of winning in view of rising Republican registrations and the increasing internal problems of the Byrd group. Holton lost to Mills E. Godwin, Jr., but he won 38 percent of the total vote to Godwin's 48 percent. When Senator Byrd announced his resignation in 1965, the Democratic organization lost the key figure in its battle to maintain unity. Harry F. Byrd, Jr., won a narrow contest in 1966 to remain in his father's old seat (to which he had been appointed the year before), but an antiorganization candidate, William B. Spong, won the Democratic primary for the other seat, ousting longtime Senator A. Willis Robertson. At the same time, veteran congressman Howard W. Smith lost a primary bid for reelection. The primary winner, George Rawlings, lost to Republican candidate William Scott in the general election in the aftermath of the Democratic in-fighting. By 1968 three wings of the old Byrd organization were identifiable, and the organization appeared to be on its last legs, as moderate Democrats jockeyed for position between the strongly pro-Byrd and anti-Byrd factions. Republicans took advantage of the breakup of the old Democratic organization, and in 1969 Holton defeated Democrat William Battle (son of the earlier state governor) in the contest for governor, after the Democrats had exhausted themselves earlier in a three-way battle for their party's nomination. Many conservative Democrats, no longer tied to the Byrd machine, actually joined the Republican party.

Other organization Democrats lost in the primary or general

Elections for Governor
(% Total Vote)

YEAR	ALABAMA Rep.	Dem.	ARKANSAS Rep.	Dem.	FLORIDA Rep.	Dem.	GEORGIA Rep.	Dem.	LOUISIANA Rep.	Dem.
1949										
1950	8.9	91.1	15.9	84.1			—	98.4		
1951										
1952			12.6	87.4	25.2	74.8			4.0	96.0
1953										
1954	26.6	73.4	37.9	62.1	19.5	80.4	—	100.0		
1955										
1956			19.4	80.6	26.3	73.7			—	100.0
1957										
1958	11.2	88.4	17.5	82.5			—	100.0		
1959										
1960			30.8	69.2	40.2	59.8			17.0	80.5
1961										
1962	—	96.3	26.7	73.3			—	99.9		
1963										
1964			43.0	57.0	41.3	56.1			38.5	60.7
1965										
1966	31.0	63.4	54.4	45.6	55.1	44.9	46.5	46.2		
1967										
1968			52.4	47.6					—	100.0
1969										
1970	—	74.5	32.4	61.7	43.1	56.9	40.6	59.3		
1971										
1972			24.6	75.6					42.8	57.2

Elections for Governor (Continued)

MISSISSIPPI		NORTH CAROLINA		SOUTH CAROLINA		TENNESSEE		TEXAS		VIRGINIA	
Rep.	Dem.	Rep.	Dem.	Rep.	Dem.	Rep.	Dem.	Rep.	Dem.	Rep.	Dem.
										27.4	70.4
				—	100.0	—	78.1	10.1	89.9		
—	100.0										
		32.5	67.5			20.6	79.4	—	98.1		
										44.3	54.8
				—	100.0	—	87.2	10.4	89.4		
—	100.0										
		33.0	67.0					14.8	78.4		
										36.4	63.2
				—	100.0	8.3	57.5	11.9	88.1		
—	100.0										
		45.5	54.4					27.2	72.8		
										36.1	63.8
				—	100.0	16.1	50.8	45.6	54.0		
38.1	61.9										
		43.4	56.6					26.0	73.8		
										37.7	47.9
				41.8	51.7	—	81.2	25.8	72.8		
29.7	70.3										
		47.3	52.7					43.0	57.0		
										52.5	45.4
				45.6	58.2	52.0	46.0	46.4	53.6		
—	77.0										
		51.0	48.5					45.0	47.9		

election, and Republicans virtually doubled their numbers in the state legislature. In 1973 Virginia's delegation to Washington contained a solid majority of Republicans over Democrats (seven to three), including Republican William Scott, who replaced incumbent William Spong to become Virginia's first GOP senator in eighty-four years. No doubt President Nixon's sweeping victory in 1972 aided Scott's move from the House to the Senate, but in truth Virginia had become a two-party state. Not a few Virginia Republicans are former Democrats who feel a closer identification with the principles of Republicanism; a prime example is Governor Godwin. This former Democratic governor served as the head of "Virginia Democrats for Nixon" in 1972, and in June of the following year Virginia Republicans picked him as their 1973 gubernatorial nominee. He won easily in November with a combination of Republican, independent, and conservative Democratic votes and was then in a position to become the architect of a fusion between the GOP and the conservative Democrats, who were being purged from the realigned Democratic party. By 1974, Virginia Republicans had the organization, size, money, and appeal necessary to make them serious opponents of the Democrats and to make Virginia a two-party state.

A faltering Democratic organization and the proliferation of Republican values aided the growth of the Republican party in Virginia; similar factors were operative in Tennessee. Politics in that state have traditionally revolved around three distinct geographic regions: the mountains of the east, the rolling hills of the middle, and the western delta land drained by the Mississippi River. Republicanism had developed in the eastern mountains in the mid-nineteenth century. Small farmers there had not supported slavery and generally had opposed secession in 1861. The events of the Civil War and Reconstruction had made them fierce Republicans, although their numbers had never been significant in statewide elections. Early in the century, Democrat E. H. Crump had built a political machine that dominated Shelby County in the western end of the state, and from a position of power in Memphis, Boss Crump and his machine joined with the middle Tennesseans to dominate the state (off and on) between 1910 and 1952; the "mountain Republicans" were generally ignored. Because Crump had always had some serious opposition, however, Tennessee was fertile ground for a genuine two-party system, especially when the machine began to crumble. In the 1950s when Republicanism began to emerge in the state's urban centers, this movement combined with the theretofore impotent eastern section to form a Republican party of considerable power. Although "mountain Republicans" had always been in the state legislature, members of their party from other regions had begun to join them, and in 1968 Republicans actually enjoyed a slim majority in the state assembly. Democrats regained control of the legislature in 1970, but in that year Republican candidates captured the governorship (Winfield Dunn) and a U.S. Senate seat (William E. Brock III), joining Republican Senator Howard Baker to give Tennessee a distinctly Republican flavor. Baker was reelected in 1972, when five of the state's eight-member delegation to Congress were elected as Republicans. The Democrats held the state legislature by the slimmest of majorities: fifty-one Democrats and forty-eight Republicans in the lower house; eighteen Democrats, fourteen Republicans, and one independent in the upper house. By no means could Tennessee be called a one-party state in 1974.

Florida's factional Democratic party was greatly affected by demographic changes. The presence of retirees and a higher per capita income encourages Republicanism in the state, although these forces have been countered by the large numbers of persons working in military- and government-related jobs. Migration, the diversified economy, the rising standard of living, and rapid urban development have combined to make Florida the most "northern" of the southern states, at the same time increasing its Republican strength. Active Florida Republicanism began in 1950, when William C. Cramer took over the party machine and helped elect Republicans to local offices as well as to the state legislature. Two years later he came close to winning a race for the U.S. House of Representatives, and in 1954, he was elected to Congress where he served for fourteen years.

The increase of Republicans in the Florida legislature tells the story of the state's growing Republicanism more than any other: in 1961, the combined houses of the state legislature had Republicans in only 8 seats of a total of 133; in 1971, Republicans held 54 of the available 165 seats. In 1966 Claude Kirk was easily elected governor, the first Republican in Florida's history since Reconstruction. But Kirk lost much of his appeal during his misadministered four-year term, and he won the Republican nomination in 1970 only after his party was badly splintered. Kirk then lost to Reubin Askew, a promising Democrat but in an increasingly Republican state. In 1968 Republican Edward J. Gurney won decisively over Democrat LeRoy Collins for U.S.

senator, this victory occurring after Republicans had not even
fielded token candidates in the Senate races as late as 1952 and
1956. Despite the Democratic comeback with new faces at the
beginning of the 1970s, everything pointed to Republicans competing fairly with their Democratic opponents in the near future.

The Republican party is less strong in North Carolina, Texas,
Arkansas, and Georgia than in Florida, Tennessee, and Virginia,
but that it is becoming a serious competitor of the Democrats
there is no doubt. Like Tennessee, North Carolina always had its
share of "mountain Republicans," and an east-west factionalism
characterized North Carolina politics until 1940. After that date
the central Piedmont began to dominate state politics. With the
development of Piedmont industry—encouraged by a string of
progressive and economy-building governors over the years—
North Carolina was invaded by northern Republicans who went
south to manage the new plants. The resultant urban growth also
added to Republican strength. Because the state as a whole
remains predominantly rural its move toward Republicanism has
been slower than most prophets foresaw. Even so, the state's
biparty competition in national elections is gaining in strength,
and this force will undoubtedly aid interparty battles at the state
and local levels. For most of the first fifty years of the twentieth
century, few Republican congressmen were included in North
Carolina's Washington delegations, and between 1930 and 1950
none were elected. Since that time, from one to four Republicans
have been regularly elected in delegations ranging from ten to
twelve members. A reapportionment plan adopted in 1971 increased the Republican advantage in seven of the eleven districts,
and a nearly even congressional delegation in the future seems
likely. In 1974 the split was seven Democrats to four Republicans.

In recent years voting statistics showed a marked increase in
the competitiveness of North Carolina's gubernatorial politics. In
1960 a relatively unknown Republican, Robert Gavin, received
45.5 percent of the vote in a race against popular Democrat Terry
Sanford, and in 1968 Republican James Gardner came within 3
percent of defeating Democrat Robert W. Scott. In 1972 the state
elected its first Republican governor (James E. Holshouser, Jr.) in
the twentieth century, and Jesse A. Helms won a surprisingly easy
Senate victory to become the state's first Republican senator in
seventy-two years. In 1972 nearly three hundred Republicans were
elected to various local offices in North Carolina, but most of
these were in the mountain regions; Republicanism was not yet

strong at the local level throughout the state. Even so, with a
Republican governor and senator and four Republicans in the
House of Representatives in 1974, Democratic one-party domi-
nance in the state was moribund.

As a part of the old Confederacy, Texas had many attributes
that were distinctly southern: a significant black population, a
cotton culture, a states' rights frame of mind, and one-party
politics. But the state's ties to the West, the size and diversity of its
landscape, its large population with various political and economic interests, and the mix of farming, ranching, and small-town
atmospheres have raised doubts as to whether Texas is "southern"
at all. In recent years Texas Democrats generally have fallen into
three loose groups: conservatives, moderates, and liberals. Texas
conservatives opposed, in order of intensity, organized labor, a
powerful national government, and government welfare spending.
By contrast, liberals favored these, but in terms of importance
they reversed the order. Most moderates were "wheeler-dealer"
politicians uncommitted to any but the most general and illusive
political philosophies. Each of the three groups have had their
share of political triumphs, conservatives or liberals usually
winning when one or the other could command the support of a
sizable bloc of moderate votes. The presence of liberal Ralph
Yarborough, moderate Price Daniel, and conservative Allan
Shivers in the same party and during the same era reveals to some
degree the complexity of Texas Democratic one-party politics.

R. B. Creager directed the weak Republican party in Texas
from 1923 to 1950. His death in 1950 coincided with economic
and social changes of great moment. The expansion of industries
(particularly those related to oil and gas and their by-products),
the rise of great metropolises, and the disillusionment of conservative Democrats with the national party boosted the Republican
party. Continued growth—particularly in the cities, among conservative wheat farmers in the Panhandle, and among long-
dissatisfied residents of the German counties of west central
Texas—resulted in some Republican candidates being forced to
win primary elections just like their Democratic counterparts. Yet
as late as 1956 one writer commented without too much exaggeration that "the Republican 'party' in Texas today could hold its
caucus in a broom closet."

A pivotal event in the life of the Republican party in Texas
was the election of Republican John Tower in 1961 for the Senate
seat vacated by Lyndon Johnson when the latter was elected

vice-president. Tower's victory, made possible by substantial
majorities in Houston, Dallas, San Antonio, Fort Worth, and El
Paso, was the first for a Republican senatorial candidate in Texas
(or the South for that matter) since Reconstruction, and it
represented a great psychological victory for Texas Republicans.
They strengthened their organization by heroic efforts, and in
1962 they nominated 273 candidates for statewide, district, and
local offices. Republican gubernatorial candidate Jack Cox received 45 percent of the votes in that year; several Republicans
were elected to the state legislature; and Republicans ran close
contests in eighteen of the state's twenty-three congressional
districts. Flamboyant, enthusiastic, and youthful conservatism
characterizes Texas Republican supporters. By 1963 the largest
and most active political organization on Austin's University of
Texas campus was the Young Republicans Club; a miniature of
the statewide picture, the campus was no longer an exclusively
Democratic preserve.

By the late 1960s and early 1970s, the Texas Democratic party
had become a bifactional arrangement composed of conservatives
(Regulars) and liberals (Loyalists). Small factions, groups, and
cliques continued to exist, but many of the old moderate,
wheeler-dealer politicians had either died (Rayburn) or retired
(Johnson), and other members of the political middle had
generally chosen sides. As distinctions grew between the two
Democratic factions and as the Republicans became a significant
force, Texas had essentially a three-party system. The gubernatorial election of 1968 reflected this arrangement. In that contest
liberal candidate Don Yarborough led in the first Democratic
primary, but he lost to Preston Smith, a colorless west Texan who
drew the conservative and moderate vote. Republican Paul Eggers
put up a losing but vigorous fight in the general election, winning
47 percent of the total vote. In 1970 Republican candidates for
governor and senator each won 46.6 percent of the vote in the
general election, after conservative Democrats had routed their
liberal opponents in the primaries. The picture in 1972 was mixed
for the Republicans. Senator Tower took 54 percent of the vote
and won a third term over moderate Democrat Barefoot
Sanders (a former aide to Lyndon Johnson) and Republican
Henry Grover of Houston won 48 percent of the vote in his race
for governor against Democrat Dolph Briscoe. As long as
conservative Democrats are firmly in the Texas saddle, the
Republican party has little chance for additional significant

growth. In 1974 Texas Republicans were not yet full competitors with the Democrats, but John Connally's switch from Democratic to Republican affiliation in May 1973 could very well alter the odds quickly if many Texans follow him into the GOP.

The liberal Democrats, once a vital force in Texas politics, have been on the wane. Briscoe's major Democratic opponent in the 1972 gubernatorial race was Frances ("Sissy") Farenthold, the liberal state senator from Corpus Christi, who won a place in the runoff primary, only to lose to the conservative rancher and great landowner. Incumbent liberal Senator Ralph Yarborough had lost his bid for reelection in the primary in 1970, and his comeback attempt failed in the primary of 1972. Yarborough's and Farenthold's losses showed that Democratic liberalism as a force in Texas had been blunted, all the more so since conservative Democrats had won most other major state offices in 1972. The future of Texas politics may depend on how effective the liberal Democrats can become. Blacks and Mexican-Americans are voting and running for office in greater numbers; if they and white liberal Democrats develop into a potent political force, conservative Democrats may be driven into league with the developing Republican party, and the state may then see a two-party system emerge after its three-party era. Prospects for a liberal revival in Texas are dim in the short run, but with the continued growth of organized labor, increased political awareness on the part of the state's two largest minorities, and the inevitable swing of the political pendulum, Texas liberals have reason for hope in the future.

For years Arkansas was the epitome of a one-party state. Factions and alliances within the Democratic party built up around individuals for each succeeding campaign, but no person or group was able to gain control of the state government for any length of time, except in the late 1950s when Governor Orval Faubus capitalized on the school desegregation crisis in Little Rock to sustain himself in office for twelve years. Urban development in the 1960s diminished Faubus's rural and segregationist support, and Arkansas was suddenly faced with a two-party possibility. Winthrop Rockefeller, who won the governorship in 1966 and 1968, was an important factor in the development of Arkansas Republicanism. In his second campaign his well-heeled and well-organized Republican organization ran a statewide slate of candidates, and thirty-seven Republicans ran for the state legislature. Rockefeller won, but lesser aspirants did not; only five

Elections to State Legislatures

STATE	LOWER HOUSE						UPPER HOUSE					
	1952		1962		1972		1952		1962		1972	
	Rep.	Dem.	Rep.	Dem.	Rep.	Dem.	Rep.	Dem.	Rep.	Dem.	Rep.	Dem.
Alabama	1	105	2	104	2	104	—	35	—	35	—	35
Arkansas	2	98	—	99	2	98	—	35	—	35	1	34
Florida	3	93	5	90	38	81	—	38	1	37	15	33
Georgia	—	205	2	203	22	173	—	54	2	52	6	50
Louisiana	—	100	—	101	1	103	—	39	—	39	1	38
Mississippi	—	140	—	140	1	120	—	49	—	49	3	49
North Carolina	10	110	21	99	24	96	2	48	2	48	7	43
South Carolina	—	125	—	124	11	113	—	46	—	46	2	42
Tennessee	19	80	21	78	43	56	4	29	6	27	13	19
Texas	1	149	7	143	10	140	—	31	—	31	2	29
Virginia	7	91	4	96	24	75	2	38	2	38	7	33

Elections to United States Congress

STATE	REPRESENTATIVES						SENATORS					
	82d Congress (1952)		87th Congress (1962)		92d Congress (1972)		82d Congress (1952)		87th Congress (1962)		92d Congress (1972)	
	Rep.	Dem.	Rep.	Dem.	Rep.	Dem.	Rep.	Dem.	Rep.	Dem.	Rep.	Dem.
Alabama	—	9	—	9	3	5	—	2	—	2	—	2
Arkansas	—	7	—	6	1	3	—	2	—	2	—	2
Florida	—	6	1	7	3	9	—	2	—	2	1	1
Georgia	—	10	—	10	2	8	—	2	—	2	—	2
Louisiana	—	8	—	8	—	8	—	2	—	2	—	2
Mississippi	—	7	—	6	—	5	—	2	—	2	—	2
North Carolina	—	12	1	11	4	7	—	2	—	2	—	2
South Carolina	—	6	—	5	1	5	—	2	—	2	1	1
Tennessee	2	8	2	7	4	5	—	2	—	2	2	—
Texas	—	21	1	19	3	20	—	2	1	1	1	1
Virginia	—	9	2	8	6	4	—	2	—	2	—	1

Republicans were elected to the legislature. Republican hopes were set back in 1970 when Rockefeller lost to Democrat Dale Bumpers and again when Republican Len Blaylock lost to Bumpers in 1972. In recent years the state has shown considerable political ambivalence. It has twice elected a Republican governor, but until 1972 it was the only southern state that had not voted Republican in at least one presidential election since Reconstruction. The Faubus spirit still survives, even though Arkansans had earlier resisted Dixiecratic appeals. A state that in 1968 elected a liberal Democratic senator (William Fulbright) and a moderate Republican governor (Rockefeller), while casting its presidential electoral votes for a racist (George Wallace) is not yet a two-party state, but neither is it solidly Democratic.

Georgia, the keystone of the southeast, has come closer to a two-party arrangement than any of the other four Deep South states. The Democrats' influence in the state in the past resulted from many factors, not the least of which was the county-unit system, which gave the state's rural regions disproportionate political leverage. This was an indirect method of nominating candidates for state office, superficially similar to the presidential electoral college. Each of the state's 159 counties had twice as many unit votes as it had members in the state House of Representatives, where the eight most populous counties were entitled to three representatives each; the next thirty, two each; and the remaining counties, one each. In order to win the party nomination for governor or U.S. senator, a candidate was required to win a majority of the county-unit votes, although all other state nominees were required to secure only a plurality. Use of this system in the Democratic primary affected every facet of Georgia politics. Candidates appealing to lightly populated, rural counties were aided by the unit rule, to the disadvantage of the city candidates. Political campaigns were intimately tied to county politics and courthouse rings. Since each county had at least one representative in the state assembly and no county had more than three, no matter how populous, the smaller Georgia counties had a disproportionate influence in the state's legislative body. When the Supreme Court demanded in *Baker* v. *Carr* (1962) that state legislatures and congressional representation be apportioned according to numerical equality within the several districts and when it invalidated the county-unit system in primary elections for statewide offices in *Gray* v. *Sanders* (1963), Georgia politics was revolutionized. Coming at a time when Georgia was more urbanized, the "one man, one vote" ruling (plus subsequent elaborative decisions) broke the rural Democratic grip on Georgia and resulted in definite signs of two-party competition.

When Georgians cast their electoral votes for Goldwater in 1964, the first time since Reconstruction that Georgia had voted for other than the Democratic nominee, the gates were opened for Georgia Republicanism. In 1966 Republican Congressman Howard ("Bo") Callaway received a plurality of 47 percent of the vote for governor, and he would have won had the Democratic-dominated state legislature not sanctioned his rival, Lester Maddox, when neither had a clear majority of the popular votes. Since Callaway had polled more popular votes than Maddox, the Republicans made the legislature's vote an advantageous issue in 1970. Georgia Republicans had other good reasons to hope for victory that year. Nixon had run second to Wallace in their state in the presidential campaign of 1968, and two Atlanta-area congressional districts had sent Republicans to Congress in 1966 and reelected them in 1968. Republicans had increased their numbers in the state legislature, and they had elected mayors to lead several of the state's medium-sized cities. In 1970 Republican Hal Suit won nearly 40 percent of the votes in his losing gubernatorial race against Jimmy Carter when the urban centers went heavily Republican. In the aftermath of the 1968 Democratic convention in Chicago, five Georgia Democrats in the state legislature had become Republicans, and in 1972 the Georgia legislature gained three additional Republicans. Republicans also won such offices as county commissioner, judge, sheriff, and school board member. In 1973 the city of Columbus elected a Republican mayor by a 68 percent majority. The Democratic primary was no longer the principal contest in Georgia. The advent of Lester Maddox on the Georgia political scene in the mid-sixties had stirred old prejudices, but by 1974 Georgia was far enough along the road to a two-party system that politically it could no longer be considered a part of the Deep South.

DEMOCRATIC HOLDOUTS

Much less progress toward a two-party system has developed in the remaining Deep South states of Alabama, Louisiana, South Carolina, and Mississippi. George Wallace won by less than his usual numbers in the 1970 Alabama gubernatorial campaign and he was confined to a wheelchair after the Maryland shooting in

March 1972; nevertheless, he retained strong personal control over state politics. His known racial views, his disenchantment with the Democratic party, and his attacks on big government dominated by eastern liberal intellectuals combined to make him appealing to alienated voters in the heart of Dixie. By competing with the Democratic party in Alabama even while he was a part of it, Wallace undercut the possibility of real growth among Republicans in the state. But this does not mean that Alabama Republicanism was nonexistent. Republican James Martin had a near-miss for a Senate seat in 1962 with 49 percent of the votes, and two of eighteen Republican candidates for the state legislature won that year. In 1964 Alabama sent no fewer than five Republican congressmen to Washington, and a sixth lost although winning 47 percent of the votes in his district. Republicans won assorted lesser local offices such as county treasurer and probate judge. Most Republican successes probably came on the coattails of Republican presidential candidate Barry Goldwater. The Republicans were encouraged, however, and they fielded more candidates in 1966, compelling Democrats to take more than passing notice of their opposition. But when the ballots were in, Republicans had fared badly: three Republican incumbent U.S. congressmen from urban areas won reelection and a GOP state senatorial candidate won, but all other nominees went down to defeat.

Alabama Republicanism fell into the doldrums after its losses in 1966, and it made little headway in the next four years. At Nixon's encouragement, in 1972 former Postmaster Winton ("Red") Blount challenged Senator John Sparkman, veteran Democrat and vice-presidential candidate in 1952. Hoping that the president's popularity would carry over to the Senate race and that the candidate of the predominantly black National Democratic party of Alabama (John LeFlore of Mobile) would take away votes from Sparkman, Blount entered the race with more than a vain chance of winning; but Sparkman turned back the challenge and dampened Republican chances in the future. Wallace's personal power and appeal—he won another term as governor in 1974—has limited the growth of the Republican party, but the flicker of interest in serious two-partyism shows that Alabama Republicanism, though far from lively, is not dead.

Since the days of Huey Long and his opponents, Louisiana politics has been notable for its bifactionalism. Within the single dominant party, Louisiana politics approximated the workings of a two-party system. But by 1974 major changes had been wrought.

Whereas political competitiveness had formerly been based on economic interest, in recent times race has forced itself into a major position. Race was overriding in Louisiana's support of the Dixiecrats in 1948, Goldwater in 1964, and Wallace in 1968. In 1952 and 1972 the state voted for Republican presidential candidates when race was not the overriding issue. Despite these voting defections from the Democratic party, only 2 percent of Louisiana voters have been registered Republicans in recent years. In 1964 Louisiana Republicans mounted a statewide campaign, running Charlton Lyons, a strong supporter of Goldwater, for governor. The Democrats beat back the Republican challenge without real difficulty, but they had faced the strongest Republican upsurge (38 percent of the votes) in nearly one hundred years. (Incidentally, both gubernatorial candidates in 1964 ran on segregationist platforms.) A definite conservative swing has been visible in state politics as black voting totals have risen. These trends have created less stability than in the past, well-illustrated in 1972 when three candidates ran for the late Allen Ellender's Senate seat. One was former governor John McKeithen, who ran as an independent after losing in the Democratic primary. Democrat J. Bennett Johnston won over McKeithen and Republican candidate Ben Toledano, but not before a real race had occurred. David Treen won a House seat, becoming the first GOP congressman from Lousiana in ninety-six years. What the future holds for Louisiana politics is anybody's guess, but the possibility of a real internal upheaval must not be discounted.

For years localism was the dominant factor in South Carolina politics. Intense interest in local issues and candidates resulted in multifactionalism within the South Carolina Democratic party. In recent times localism has lessened, mainly due to the influence of mass media and better transportation throughout the state. Broader interests within the state have brought on more statewide political competition, which should rid the state of much of its local factionalism. But this does not necessarily mean a growth of Republicanism.

The presence of black voters in the Democratic party has driven some whites into league with the Republicans, but the ultimate consequences of these moves are yet to be seen. In 1962 Republican W. D. Workman, Jr., received 42.8 percent of the vote in his losing race for the Senate against incumbent Olin Johnston. In 1966 Democrat Ernest Hollings won a special Senate race over Republican Marshall Parker by only 11,758 votes. But these developments and Senator Thurmond's and Congressman Albert Watson's moves from Democratic to Republican affiliation constituted neither a permanent massive shift among South Carolina voters nor strengthening of a state Republican organization. In 1950, 1954, 1958, and 1962 the Democratic nominees for governor faced no Republican opponents in the general elections. From 1948 to 1968 Republican candidates entered a total of only six statewide elections in South Carolina, Thurmond being the single Republican victor during that time. In 1961 a Republican was elected to the South Carolina legislature, the first since the turn of the century, and in 1966, twenty-three Republicans were elected to a variety of local offices, mostly from urban areas. Many of these gains were lost in 1968, however, and in 1972 Democrats swept the state offices, except for two Republican congressmen and Thurmond. An encouraging straw in the wind for the GOP was seen in 1973 when the city of Greenville elected Republicans to four county and city council positions. Pointing up the reality of political power, Thurmond bid for black votes in his 1972 race for another term. The role of the black man in the politics and economy of the state may yet have more influence upon the future makeup of the political structure of South Carolina than concepts such as states' rights, conservatism, and status quo.

Mississippi in 1974 was the most rural of the southern states; it had the largest percentage of blacks (37 percent); and it was the most economically depressed. Historically these factors have dominated the politics of the state, and they continue to do so today. Blacks are more involved in the political process than before, but thus far this involvement has not been strong enough to force white Mississippians to wipe "racial politics" from an uppermost position in their minds during elections and on voting days. Indeed, some evidence indicates that black political participation has hardened white thinking and that Mississippians are more than ever concerned with the "specter of color." Blacks in the state have joined the Democratic party, but thus far their influence has been slight in the face of racist whites. White Democrats are not moving out of the Democratic party in large numbers, but they have been willing to forego party label on election day to vote for a Wallace, a Goldwater, a Nixon, or local candidates who continue to ride racist themes overtly or covertly. The dormant Republican party has attempted to be a factor in state politics since the early 1950s, but it has been little rewarded for its efforts. In 1963 Republican gubernatorial candidate Rubel

Phillips of Jackson won more than 38 percent of the votes, but the unprecedented 87 percent of the popular vote racked up by Goldwater in the election the following year made few permanent converts to the Republican party in Mississippi. Republican hopes rose a little in 1964 when Prentiss Walker won a House seat, the first Mississippi GOP congressman in the twentieth century. He ran against Senator Eastland in 1966, but he and other Republican hopefuls were defeated decisively. The party fell upon hard times when these losses were repeated two years later. In 1972 Eastland easily survived the challenge of three opponents (one Republican and two independents, one of the latter being Walker), partly because Eastland's opponents took votes from each other. President Nixon won 80 percent of the state's vote in 1972, and the U.S. House delegation from Mississippi in 1973 was composed of three Democrats and two Republicans. On the local scene the Mississippi GOP was jubilant when in 1973 Republicans scored their greatest gains of the century: they won 63 of the 140 council and mayoralty positions on the ballot, including a net gain of 12 mayors. These results were perhaps indicators of the future. Although the presence of blacks, economic change, and alienation from the national party are bringing about changes in Mississippi's Democratic party, one-party politics is not about to die.

Three of the formerly solid Democratic southern states—Virginia, Tennessee, and perhaps Florida—have viable two-party systems. North Carolina, Texas, Arkansas, and Georgia are nearing the end of one-party dominance while Alabama, Louisiana, and South Carolina, although still primarily Democratic, have unstable political situations that could rapidly move their state Republican parties to positions of competitiveness under the right conditions. Mississippi stands alone as having made minimum progress toward two-party politics in the twentieth century. Because of social, economic, demographic, and psychological factors, politics in the several southern states has been altered drastically in modern times. In all likelihood these factors will accelerate political change in the future.

THE FUTURE OF
POLITICS IN THE
AMERICAN SOUTH

Throughout most of the years of the twentieth century, southern Democrats had a viselike grip on major positions in

Congress. Even in the past twenty years approximately a third of the House Democratic delegation came from southern districts, and generally more than that representation obtained in the Senate, placing these long-tenured and numerous southerners in powerful committee chairmanships in both houses. In the past two decades, at no time have southern Democrats chaired less than a majority of the House's standing committees, and the percentage has been almost as high for the Senate. In 1963, for example, twenty-three of the thirty-six standing committees in the Senate and House had southern Democrats as chairmen, and on twenty-three committees the second-ranking member was a southern Democrat. Death, retirement, and an occasional lost election cut into the strength of these southern titans, but those remaining continued to wield power.

The development of Republican parties in the southern states, however, has now begun to affect the political makeup of their delegations to Congress. As late as 1960 no Republican senators and only seven Republican congressmen served the South, out of 126 seats in both houses. As a result of the 1972 elections the new Congress included 34 Republicans out of 105 southern House positions; every southern state delegation had at least one Republican member. Of the twenty-two senatorial seats occupied by southerners, one was held by an independent (Harry F. Byrd, Jr.) and Republicans filled no fewer than seven (Tower of Texas, Thurmond of South Carolina, Baker and Brock of Tennessee, Gurney of Florida, Helms of North Carolina, and Scott of Virginia). If these southern Republicans can remain in office—and this is certainly likely for many of them—they may become as powerful in the national legislature as were southern Democrats in years gone by, because the committee seniority system places a premium on longevity.

How have these new southern Republicans voted on issues of local, state, and national import?

Several broad issues of public policy have confronted Congress in recent years, the most important being civil rights for blacks; domestic economic and social policies, including social welfare, economic regulation, housing, labor, and education; civil liberties; and foreign policy. Both Democratic and Republican southerners have stubbornly opposed more civil rights for blacks. As the civil rights movement gained momentum, fewer northern Republicans voted with the southerners to oppose civil rights legislation, and in this area the southern Democrats and Republicans have been left without important support. In the other three major areas of concern, southerners and northern Republicans in Washington have worked together in a conservative coalition. They have expressed hostility to urban social and welfare programs, opposed increased spending and growth of the federal government, and desired state control over government programs. In regard to civil liberties, this coalition opposed northern Democratic attempts to cut off funds for the House Committee on Un-American Activities and the Subversive Activities Control Board. In foreign affairs the bipartisan conservative coalition desired to reduce foreign aid. The internationalism favored by southerners in an earlier era was by now almost a sinister term. The South's increasing industrialization has made the section less dependent upon cotton and tobacco exports, and its representatives have correspondingly given less support to reciprocal trade agreements. Southerners' stands have been conservative on most issues facing the nation, not just civil rights for blacks even though their strongest objections have been raised in that area.

The idea of a conservative coalition opposing liberals on labor issues, minimum wages, social programs, heavy spending, and "big government" started in the days when conservative southern Democrats revolted against Roosevelt and the New Deal. Recently, when the Nixon administration began to run into such difficulties as the Watergate break-in and cover-up, the confirmation of a new director for the FBI, and the ITT affair, a Democrat, Senator Eastland, became one of President Nixon's most ardent defenders, in some instances actually playing the part of a Nixon wheelhorse—a disturbing irony to many Democrats. After 1969 Eastland controlled much of the Nixon administration's Mississippi patronage, and as chairman of the august Senate Judiciary Committee he often worked closely with Nixon's attorney general. Arkansas's John McClellan, the second-ranking Democrat on the Judiciary Committee, also worked with the White House and the Justice Department. There was continued speculation that Eastland and Virginia's Democrat-turned-Independent Byrd were about to become official Republicans.

Presidential politics certainly were affecting southern politics. The white southerner's racial prejudices had driven him away from Truman in 1948 and pulled him toward Goldwater in 1964. In the 1972 campaign Nixon's not so subtle opposition to school integration and busing did not go unnoticed by southerners long adept at recognizing racist code words. The strength of presiden-

'We'd Better Start Learnin' Dixie!'

Don Hesse, *The St. Louis Globe-Democrat*, 1972

tial Republicanism rests upon more than Republican appeals to race or southern Democrats' protests against their party's national stand in favor of racial progress. Many southerners have long held a political philosophy on other issues closer to mainstream Republicanism than mainstream Democratic politics. Conservative southerners and the majority of national Republicans have for years shared such notions as more power for state governments, less national spending, sympathy for business, low taxes, dislike of organized labor, limited welfare programs. Eisenhower's appeal in the South was greatest among upper-income whites, small businessmen, white-collar workers, industrial managers. Logic dictates that these southerners should vote Republican in presidential elections, and (after breaking tradition) that they also should vote Republican in lesser elections. A shift of party registration would be the final step. Such switches will not be easy for longtime Democrats; psychological adherence is still strong in the South, and the vast majority of southern whites retain their emotional identification as Democrats even though some of them have not supported a Democratic presidential candidate for nearly two decades. The weight of history militates against a reorientation of the party structure along ideological lines. But all the ingredients for such a change are present and the next generation may see it.

The Republican party in the South has a great deal of potential support. It can count on immigrants from the North and new, young, white voters. Northerners have gone South to fill managerial and professional positions, and young conservative voters are less impressed by tradition today than they were a quarter of a century ago. Added to these groups are the large numbers of middle-class southern families whose incomes and standards of living have helped them identify with Republicanism. These groups of voters constitute a reservoir for the party, if it will only rally its supporters. But national Republican leaders thus far have been shortsighted. They have been more interested in winning presidential elections than in developing a two-party South. Furthermore, if they continue their appeals to white southerners on the basis of race, they will jeopardize the future of the national Republican party which in recent years has become more liberal on racial progress. Since economic conservatism and racial prejudice do not always go together in the South, the Republicans should be very careful to make their appeal on the basis of economic interests.

Upper-class white Democrats have not yet changed their

registrations in appreciable numbers, but as time passes that could occur, particularly as these economic conservatives become disenchanted with the Democratic party and pay correspondingly less attention to party label. Here is a large group of southerners who are ready for Republicanism, and the national party would do well to recognize its opportunity. The Southern Establishment is not likely to turn to the GOP overnight ("The Republican tide is sweeping over Dixie at glacial speed"), but its prospects should not be dismissed lightly. The transition of Virginia, Tennessee, and Florida from one-party politics to genuine two-party arrangements will be followed by other southern states as social and economic change spreads through the South. Important in this realignment will be the role of the black voter.

In terms of organized politics, politically sensitive blacks have had three choices at the state level: to establish separate, predominantly black third parties; to join the growing but still small Republican party; to join the still dominant Democratic party. Some blacks attempted to organize third parties based on race, but these were not widely supported.

As the Republican party increased its white numbers south of the Potomac, conceivably blacks could have joined it to provide southern states with the reality of a two-party system. In the distant past, southern blacks had traditionally been Republicans, out of respect for the Great Emancipator and in reaction to white supremacists who dominated state Democratic party organizations in the South. Furthermore, the southern Democrats' emphasis upon states' rights offended those blacks who looked to the national government in Washington for assistance in their cause. But the social welfare and economic programs provided by the Democrats in the 1930s and thereafter nudged black voters in the direction of the Democratic party, and when southern blacks began to register in greater numbers in the postwar period, they generally joined the national party they respected, even though it meant allying themselves with white southerners, their former enemies.

At least they could have more influence if they joined the majority party. In most of the southern states the blacks have been absorbed into the state Democratic political organization, working with whites and using whatever power they can muster to gain concessions for their race.

White determination to ban black political activity was still present in the South in 1974, and it is not likely to end soon even though the barriers continue to fall. Economic pressure, custom, fear on the part of the black, and white administration of primary machinery still prevent many blacks from voting. In the heat of the civil rights movement, the greatest detriment to black voting is the black himself. In a region not known for high voting ratios, even among whites, blacks have not been trained in their responsibilities in citizenship. If all barriers to blacks were suddenly removed, many qualified blacks would still fail to vote. The southern black is not yet a significant part of the American democratic political process. At the same time, no doubt blacks will emerge as a considerable force in politically liberalizing congressional districts and metropolitan areas. A durable coalition between white and black voters in the South is a distinct possibility, and it holds more promise than did similar political cooperation between the two races during the Reconstruction and Populist eras.

Not beyond the realm of possibility is a Democratic party in the southern states comprised primarily of black and white moderates and liberals, while economic conservatives migrate to the Republican party. As racial tensions diminish, racial politics may someday be passé, and party affiliations in the South will be realigned on the basis of economic interest. White southern segregationists will be left without influential champions in either national party.

What then does the future hold for southern politics and politicians—and for the people of the American South, both blacks and whites? The growth of metropolitan centers, continued migration of whites from the North, development of industry, the effect of federal expenditures, the sprawl of suburbia, the decline of rural dwellers, the rising standards of living, the presence of the black southerner in both voting booths and political offices, the pressure of the national party system, the push of southern Republicanism, the new relations of whites and blacks in society and economics, the rise of a new generation within the South, and many other changes and influences: all these will have their individual and collective imprint upon southern politics. If the phrase "the changing South" has become a cliché, it nonetheless describes accurately the politics of the South. Southern politics have changed markedly in the immediate past, are changing now, and surely will continue to change into the long future.

Bibliographical
Essay
Sources for the study of politics in the twentieth century are numerous. For the immediate past, I have relied heavily upon contemporary newspapers and news magazines. Articles in scholarly journals and government documents (including the *Congressional Record*) constitute other important sources. Historians and political scientists have written many books on specific topics, and I have leaned upon these secondary sources for many sections of this volume. The following essay is designed not only to reveal some of the more significant books that I have used, but also to make readily available a list for those who would like to read beyond this brief synthesis. The volumes marked with an asterisk (*) are available in paperback.

GENERAL WORKS

V. O. Key, Jr., *Southern Politics in State and Nation** (New York: Knopf, 1949), is the classic beginning for any study of southern politics in the first half of the twentieth century. Equally valuable is Key's *American State Politics* (New York: Knopf, 1956). William C. Havard, editor, *The Changing Politics of the*

South (Baton Rouge: Louisiana State University Press, 1972), is a lengthy, multiauthor, state-by-state account updating Key's works on southern politics. The chapters are well researched and their conclusions are well grounded, and Havard has written a sound introduction as well as a perceptive conclusion. C. Vann Woodward, *Origins of the New South, 1877–1913** (Baton Rouge: Louisiana State University Press, 1951), and George B. Tindall, *The Emergence of the New South, 1913–1945** (Baton Rouge: Louisiana State University Press, 1967), survey the entirety of southern history and contain excellent chapters on politics. T. Harry Williams, *Romance and Realism in Southern Politics** (Athens: University of Georgia Press, 1961); Dewey W. Grantham, Jr., *The Democratic South** (Athens: University of Georgia Press, 1963); and George B. Tindall, *The Disruption of the Solid South** (Athens: University of Georgia Press, 1972), are filled with sagacious comments about developments in the twentieth-century political South. Two other recent general studies are George E. Mowry, *Another Look at the Twentieth-Century South* (Baton Rouge: Louisiana State University Press, 1973), and David M. Potter, *The South and the Concurrent Majority* (Baton Rouge: Louisiana State University Press, 1972). Older general works not to be overlooked include Jasper B. Shannon, *Toward a New Politics in the South* (Knoxville: University of Tennessee Press, 1949); Cortez A. M. Ewing, *Congressional Elections, 1896–1944: The Sectional Basis of Political Democracy in the House of Representatives* (Norman: University of Oklahoma Press, 1947); Alexander Heard, *A Two-Party South?* (Chapel Hill: University of North Carolina Press, 1952); and Wilbur J. Cash, *The Mind of the South** (New York: Random House, 1941). Samuel Lubell's works contain many references to the South: *The Future of American Politics** (New York: Harper and Row, 1952); *Revolt of the Moderates* (New York: Harper and Row, 1956); *White and Black: Test of a Nation** (New York: Harper and Row, 1964); and *The Hidden Crisis in American Politics** (New York: Norton, 1970). Finally, material on southerners and foreign policy may be found in Alfred O. Hero, Jr., *The Southerner and World Affairs* (Baton Rouge: Louisiana State University Press, 1965), and Charles O. Lerche, Jr., *The Uncertain South* (Chicago: Quadrangle Books, 1964).

FROM 1900 TO 1930

Much has been written about southern politics during the Progressive era. Jack Temple Kirby, *Darkness at the Dawning: Race and Reform in the Progressive South** (Philadelphia: Lippincott, 1972), is a recent study showing that racism was central to the reforms of the southern Progressives. Reinhard Luthin, *American Demagogues: Twentieth Century* (Boston: Beacon Press, 1954), and Allan A. Michie and Frank Rhylick, *Dixie Demagogues* (New York: Vanguard, 1939), are critical of some of the South's early political leaders, while Albert D. Kirwan, *Revolt of the Rednecks: Mississippi Politics, 1876–1925* (Lexington: University of Kentucky Press, 1951), in a pioneering scholarly study, plays down racial demagoguery and plays up the progressivism of Mississippi's leaders in the early years of the twentieth century. Material on the role of southerners in national politics may be found in Arthur S. Link, *Woodrow Wilson and the Progressive Era, 1910–1917** (New York: Harper and Row, 1954), as well as in Link's incomplete multivolume biography of Woodrow Wilson (Princeton: Princeton University Press, 1947–).

David Bruner, *The Politics of Provincialism: The Democratic Party in Transition, 1918–1932* (New York: Knopf, 1968), is valuable for the years it considers, chapter six being a particularly good account of the activities and influence of the congressional Democrats in the 1920s. Volumes rich in information about Huey Long and Louisiana are: T. Harry Williams, *Huey Long** (New York: Knopf, 1969); Allan P. Sindler, *Huey Long's Louisiana: State Politics, 1920–1952** (Baltimore: Johns Hopkins University Press, 1956); and Stan Opotowsky, *The Longs of Louisiana* (New York: Dutton, 1960). Jack Temple Kirby, *Westmoreland Davis: Virginia Planter-Politician, 1859–1942* (Charlottesville: University of Virginia Press, 1968), describes the southern politician as reformer in the 1920s.

Volumes devoted wholly or partially to the political implications of the antievolution controversy include Norman F. Furniss, *The Fundamentalist Controversy, 1918–1931* (New Haven: Yale University Press, 1954); Willard B. Gatewood, Jr., *Preachers, Pedagogues and Politicians: The Evolution Controversy in North Carolina, 1920–1927* (Chapel Hill: University of North Carolina Press, 1966); and Kenneth K. Bailey's unpublished work, "The Antievolution Crusade of the Nineteen-Twenties" (Ph.D. dissertation, Vanderbilt University, 1953). David M. Chalmers, *Hooded Americanism: The First Century of the Ku Klux Klan, 1865–1965** (Garden City, N.Y.: Doubleday, 1965), is a good general study of the Klan. Charles C. Alexander, *The Ku Klux Klan in the Southwest** (Lexington: University of Kentucky Press, 1965), studies the hooded order in the 1920s in Texas, Oklahoma, Arkansas, and Louisiana. Arnold S. Rice, *The Ku Klux Klan in American Politics* (Washington, D.C.: Public Affairs Press, 1962), examines the political activities of the revived Klan on both local and national levels. Kenneth T. Jackson's *The Ku Klux Klan in the City, 1915–1930** (New York: Oxford University Press, 1967), contains much material devoted to the urban South.

THE THIRTIES AND
FORTIES

Frank Freidel's volume *F.D.R. and the South** (Baton Rouge: Louisiana State University Press, 1965) is a slim but good beginning for studying the political South during the 1930s. James T. Patterson, *Congressional Conservatism and the New Deal: The Growth of the Conservative Coalition in Congress, 1933–1939** (Lexington: University of Kentucky Press, 1967), is an excellent study of the New Deal era. James E. Palmer, Jr., *Carter Glass, Unreconstructed Rebel* (Roanoke, Va.: Institute of American Biography, 1938), and G. C. Osborn, *John Sharp Williams* (Baton Rouge: Louisiana State University Press, 1943), are biographies pertinent to the New Deal. Information on the New Deal and the southern states may also be found in Roy Edward Fossett, "The Impact of the New Deal on Georgia Politics, 1933–1941" (Ph.D. dissertation, University of Florida, 1960); John Dean Minton, "The New Deal in Tennessee, 1932–1938" (Ph.D. dissertation, Vanderbilt University, 1959); and Lionel V. Patenaude, "The New Deal in Texas" (Ph.D. dissertation, University of Texas, 1953). Of less value but worth mentioning are Elmer L. Puryear, *Democratic Party Dissension in North Carolina, 1928–1936** (Chapel Hill: University of North Carolina Press, 1962); William D. Miller, *Mr. Crump of Memphis* (Baton Rouge: Louisiana State Univeristy Press, 1964); and Seth Shepard McKay, *W. Lee O'Daniel and Texas Politics, 1938–1942* (Lubbock: Texas Tech University Press, 1944).

Cabell Phillips, *The Truman Presidency: The History of a Triumphant Succession* (New York: Macmillan, 1966), is a detailed

story with much material on the South and southerners. James F.
Byrnes, a South Carolinian who served for over fifty years in all
three branches of the national government, was active during the
Truman administration as he reveals in his autobiography, *All in
One Lifetime* (New York: Harper and Row, 1958). William C.
Berman, *The Politics of Civil Rights in the Truman Administration*
(Columbus: Ohio State University Press, 1970), is of great value
for studying the relationships of Truman, the South, and blacks.
Emile B. Ader, *The Dixiecrat Movement: Its Role in Third Party
Politics* (Washington, D.C.: Public Affairs Press, 1955), is a
concise study of the States' Rights party of 1948. On this subject
see also the final essay in Barton J. Bernstein, editor, *Politics and
Policies of the Truman Administration** (Chicago: Quadrangle
Books, 1970). Ellis G. Arnall, *The Shore Dimly Seen* (Philadelphia:
Lippincott, 1946), expresses the opinions of an active southern
politician in the immediate postwar era. Helpful but too laudatory
is Alberta Lachicotte, *Rebel Senator: Strom Thurmond of South
Carolina* (Greenwich, Conn.: Devin-Adair, 1966). A recently
published biography is Joseph Bruce Gorman's *Kefauver* (New
York: Oxford University Press, 1971).

BLACKS IN POLITICS

The South's preoccupation with the role of blacks on the
political scene is well recounted in Paul Lewinson, *Race, Class,
and Party: A History of Negro Suffrage and White Politics in the
South** (New York: Oxford University Press, 1932). Harry A.
Bailey, Jr., editor, *Negro Politics in America** (Columbus, Ohio:
Charles E. Merrill, 1967), contains essays originally published in
scholarly journals or in recent monographs. The chapters on the
South are well researched and contain useful analyses of the
political status of the South. A recent volume based on research in
Tuskegee, Alabama, and Durham, North Carolina, has much to
say about the entire South: William R. Keech, *The Impact of
Negro Voting: The Role of the Vote in the Quest for Equality*
(Chicago: Rand McNally, 1968). Chuck Stone, *Black Political
Power in America** (Indianapolis: Bobbs-Merrill, 1968), has a
fact-filled chapter on the South, but Stone's contention that blacks
will be more influential if they form third parties appears
unrealistic for the South. Pertinent is Pat Watters and Reece
Cleghorn, *Climbing Jacob's Ladder: The Arrival of Negroes in
Southern Politics** (New York: Harcourt Brace Jovanovich, 1967).

Brief pamphlets of value by Margaret Price are "The Negro Voter in the South" (Atlanta: Southern Regional Council, 1957) and "The Negro and the Ballot in the South" (Atlanta: Southern Regional Council, 1959). An informative study is Elbert L. Tatum's *The Changed Political Thought of the Negro, 1915–1940* (New York: Exposition, 1951). Contending that the poll tax was not the chief method for black disfranchisement is Frederick D. Ogden, *The Poll Tax in the South* (University: University of Alabama Press, 1958). Not as politically oriented but valuable nevertheless is C. Vann Woodward's *The Strange Career of Jim Crow,** 3rd rev. ed. (New York: Oxford University Press, 1974).

A case study of one southern state with wider implications for the entire South is Hugh D. Price, *The Negro and Southern Politics: A Chapter of Florida History* (New York: New York University Press, 1957). A sound study of recent political developments in Houston, Texas, the South's largest city, is Chandler Davidson, *Biracial Politics: Conflict and Coalition in the Metropolitan South* (Baton Rouge: Louisiana State University Press, 1972). Davidson argues persuasively that to protect and advance their interests blacks have little alternative but to cooperate with the white political establishment. More general but with major implications for the future of southern politics is Harry Holloway, *The Politics of the Southern Negro: From Exclusion to Big City Organization* (New York: Random House, 1969). Also available is Donald S. Strong's slim volume limited to the years from 1957 to 1965 entitled *Negroes, Ballots, and Judges: National Voting Rights Legislation in the Federal Courts* (University: University of Alabama Press, 1968). Donald R. Matthews and James W. Prothro, *Negroes and the New Southern Politics* (New York: Harcourt Brace Jovanovich, 1968), is a detailed study based on extensive interviews and contains much valuable information. Charles Wallace Collins, *Whither Solid South? A Study in Politics and Race Relations* (New Orleans: Pelican, 1947), is flawed by the author's bias against blacks and for white southerners; nevertheless much important material is included. Of more value are Andrew Buni, *The Negro in Virginia Politics, 1902–1965* (Charlottesville: University of Virginia Press, 1967), and Numan V. Bartley, *The Rise of Massive Resistance: Race and Politics in the South during the 1950's* (Baton Rouge: Louisiana State University Press, 1969). Frederick M. Wirt, *Politics of Southern Equality: Law and Social Change in a Mississippi County* (Chicago: Aldine, 1970), deals with the effects of recent federal civil rights legislation on the behavior and

attitudes of the inhabitants of Panola County, Mississippi. The
section on voting is worthwhile, since it is instructive for the whole
of Mississippi and the South as well. Three other case studies with
ramifications for the region are: Everett Carll Ladd, Jr., *Negro
Political Leadership in the South** (Ithaca, N.Y.: Cornell University Press, 1966), which focuses on Winston-Salem, North Carolina, and Greenville, South Carolina; Daniel C. Thompson, *The
Negro Leadership Class* (Englewood Cliffs, N.J.: Prentice-Hall,
1963), which is a study of black leaders and the decision-making
function in New Orleans; and Margaret E. Burgess, *Negro
Leadership in a Southern City** (Chapel Hill: University of North
Carolina Press, 1960), which studies "Cresent City," a real but
unnamed urban center in the Middle South.

Harry Golden, *Mr. Kennedy and the Negroes** (New York:
Fawcett World Library, 1964), deals primarily with the South and
relates favorably the story of black advancement during the
Kennedy years. More objective is James C. Harvey, *Civil Rights
During the Kennedy Administration* (Hattiesburg, Miss.: University
and College Press of Mississippi, 1971), a brief, tentative, but
well-documented study that sketches the main outlines of the
subject of its title. James W. Silver, *Mississippi: The Closed
Society** (New York: Harcourt Brace Jovanovich, 1964), is a
firsthand observer's story of the integration of the University of
Mississippi. The role of the Kennedy administration and southern
politicians in the campus violence is not overlooked. James L.
Sundquist, *Politics and Policy: The Eisenhower, Kennedy and
Johnson Years** (Washington, D.C.: The Brookings Institution,
1968), has a good chapter on civil rights during the Kennedy and
Johnson administrations. A more recent publication mainly
covering the decade of the sixties is Allan Wolk, *The Presidency
and Black Civil Rights: Eisenhower to Nixon* (Rutherford, N.J.:
Fairleigh Dickinson University Press, 1971).

SOUTHERN REPUB-
LICANISM

Alan F. Westin, editor, *The Uses of Power: Seven Cases in
American Politics** (New York: Harcourt Brace Jovanovich, 1962),
includes a chapter entitled "The Unsolid South: A Challenge to
the Democratic Party," covering the period from 1948 to 1960
when Republican gains in the South first became noticeable. John
G. Topping, Jr., John R. Lazarek, and William H. Hinder,

Southern Republicanism and the New South (Cambridge, Mass.: Republicans for Progress and the Ripon Society, 1966), addresses a specific phenomenon in southern politics. An exhaustive account of preconvention politics in 1952, a pivotal election in both national and sectional politics, is Paul T. David, Malcolm Moos, and Ralph M. Goldman, *Presidential Nominating Politics in 1952*, 5 vols. (Baltimore: Johns Hopkins University Press, 1954). See especially volume 3, *The South.* Useful material may be found in Donald S. Strong, *Urban Republicanism in the South* (University: University of Alabama Bureau of Public Administration, 1960), which focuses on the 1956 presidential election. This little volume is filled with insights, and the events of the decade of the 1960s proved the author correct in his comments on the correlation of urbanism and Republicanism in the South. The role of the South is detailed in the presidential campaign histories of Theodore H. White: *The Making of the President, 1960** (New York: Atheneum, 1961); *The Making of the President, 1964** (New York: Atheneum, 1965); *The Making of the President, 1968** (New York: Atheneum, 1969); *The Making of the President, 1972** (New York: Atheneum, 1973). Of value is Bernard Cosman, *Five States for Goldwater: Continuity and Change in Southern Presidential Voting Patterns, 1920–1964* (University: University of Alabama Press, 1966). Broader than the title suggests, this book is statistically oriented and concerned with voter behavior. Cosman has also published *The Case of the Goldwater Delegates* (University: University of Alabama Bureau of Public Administration, 1966), and with Robert J. Huckshorn he has edited *Republican Politics: The 1964 Campaign and Its Aftermath for the Party* (New York: Praeger, 1968). Also worthy of a notation are Robert D. Novak, *The Agony of the G.O.P. 1964* (New York: Macmillan, 1965); George F. Gilder and Bruce K. Chapman, *The Party that Lost Its Head* (New York: Knopf, 1966); Stephen Hess and David S. Broder, *The Republican Establishment: The Present and Future of the GOP* (New York: Harper and Row, 1967); and John H. Kessel, *The Goldwater Coalition: Republican Strategies in 1964** (Indianapolis: Bobbs-Merrill, 1968). Not to be overlooked is Lewis Chester, Godfrey Hodgson, and Bruce Page, *An American Melodrama: The Presidential Campaign of 1968** (New York: Viking, 1969).

Avery Leiserson, editor, *The American South in the 1960s* (New York: Praeger, 1964), has much valuable material on politics. Two books tell a great deal about George Wallace's entry upon the national political scene: Marshall Frady, *Wallace** (New York:

World, 1968); W. G. Jones, *The Wallace Story* (Montgomery, Ala.: American South Publishers, 1966). Much more critical is the essay on Wallace by Robert Sherrill in his *Gothic Politics in the Deep South: Stars of the New Confederacy** (New York: Grossman, 1968). The latter volume has lively, brief biographies of several other recent southern politicians as well. Zeroing in on Richard Nixon and his relationship to the South is Reg Murphy and Harold Gulliver, *The Southern Strategy** (New York: Scribners, 1971), a revealing—and perhaps overly critical—account of the Nixon administration's attempts to appeal for southern support. Kevin Phillips, *The Emerging Republican Majority** (New Rochelle, N.Y.: Arlington House, 1969), argues that the future of the Republican party lies in its appeal to the nation's conservative suburbs, the South, the "Sunbelt" (from southern California to Florida), and the white, Catholic labor force. According to Phillips these groups and regions—conspicuously absent are the liberals and the Northeast—could coalesce under the Republican banner to replace the old Roosevelt coalition of the 1930s that dominated American political life for so long. Phillips's major thesis is that the South is turning into an important presidential base for the Republican party. Finally, emphasizing the possibility of political fragmentation in the nation and the South is Frederick G. Dutton, *Changing Sources of Power: American Politics in the 1970s** (New York: McGraw-Hill, 1971).

RECENT STATE POLITICS

Giving attention to recent state politics are: Numan V. Bartley, *From Thurmond to Wallace: Political Tendencies in Georgia, 1948–1968** (Baltimore: Johns Hopkins University Press, 1970); Francis Pickens Miller, *Man from the Valley: Memoirs of a 20th-Century Virginian* (Chapel Hill: University of North Carolina Press, 1971); J. Harvie Wilkinson III, *Harry F. Byrd and the Changing Face of Virginia Politics, 1945–1966* (Charlottesville: University of Virginia Press, 1968); and Harold M. Hollingsworth, editor, *Essays on Recent Southern Politics* (Austin: University of Texas Press, 1970). William C. Havard and Loren P. Beth, *The Politics of Mis-Representation: Rural-Urban Conflict in the Florida Legislature* (Baton Rouge: Louisiana State University Press, 1962), is an excellent study focusing on Florida politics but which in fact has wide implications for the entire South. Joseph L. Bernd, *Grass Roots Politics in Georgia: The County Unit System* *and the Importance of the Individual Voting Community in Bifactional Elections, 1942–1954* (Atlanta: Emory University Research Committee, 1960), and L. M. Holland, *The Direct Primary in Georgia Politics* (Norman: University of Oklahoma Press, 1953), complement each other well. Malcolm E. Jewell, editor, *The Politics of Reapportionment* (Englewood Cliffs, N.J.: Prentice-Hall, 1962), has chapters on several southern states. James Reichley, *States in Crisis: Politics in Ten American States, 1950–1962* (Chapel Hill: University of North Carolina Press, 1964), has a chapter on Virginia, mainly concerned with political events surrounding the 1954 Supreme Court decision. It also has a lucid chapter on Texas politics, detailing intraparty battles as well as pointing out the prospects for a growing Republican party there. Dealing with rising Republicanism in Texas, as well as that state's liberal-conservative Democratic split, is James R. Soukup, Clifton McCleskey, and Harry Holloway, *Party and Factional Division in Texas** (Austin: University of Texas Press, 1964). Also important are Malcolm E. Jewell, *Legislative Representation in the Contemporary South* (Durham, N.C.: Duke University Press, 1967), and Allan P. Sindler, editor, *Change in the Contemporary South* (Durham, N.C.: Duke University Press, 1963), which has essays on subjects such as black voter registration in the South, rising southern Republicanism, and changes on the local southern political scene.

Index

Index

199